D1311730

The Art of

X²

The Art of X2

A NEWMARKET PICTORIAL MOVIEBOOK

DESIGNED AND EDITED BY
TIMOTHY SHANER

NEWMARKET PRESS
NEW YORK

New Hanover County Public Library
201 Chestnut Street
Wilmington, NC 28401

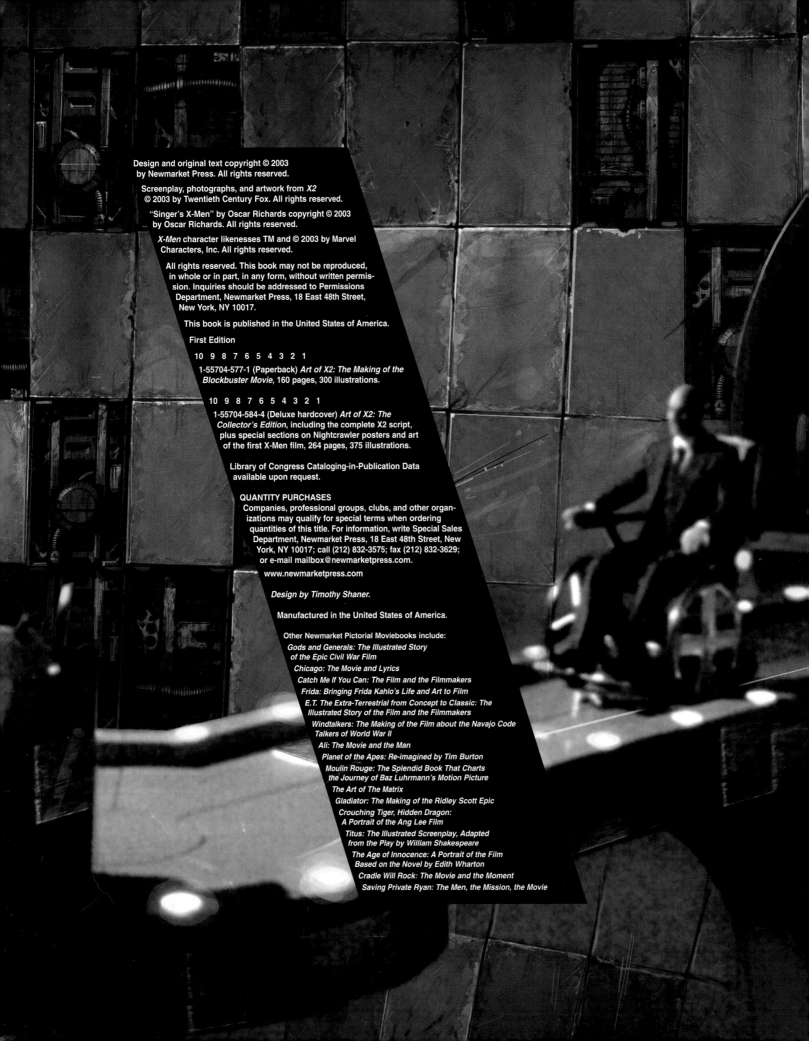

Design and original text copyright © 2003
by Newmarket Press. All rights reserved.

Screenplay, photographs, and artwork from *X2*
© 2003 by Twentieth Century Fox. All rights reserved.

"Singer's X-Men" by Oscar Richards copyright © 2003
by Oscar Richards. All rights reserved.

X-Men character likenesses TM and © 2003 by Marvel
Characters, Inc. All rights reserved.

All rights reserved. This book may not be reproduced,
in whole or in part, in any form, without written permis-
sion. Inquiries should be addressed to Permissions
Department, Newmarket Press, 18 East 48th Street,
New York, NY 10017.

This book is published in the United States of America.

First Edition

10 9 8 7 6 5 4 3 2 1

1-55704-577-1 (Paperback) *Art of X2: The Making of the
Blockbuster Movie*, 160 pages, 300 illustrations.

10 9 8 7 6 5 4 3 2 1

1-55704-584-4 (Deluxe hardcover) *Art of X2: The
Collector's Edition*, including the complete X2 script,
plus special sections on Nightcrawler posters and art
of the first X-Men film, 264 pages, 375 illustrations.

Library of Congress Cataloging-in-Publication Data
available upon request.

QUANTITY PURCHASES
Companies, professional groups, clubs, and other organ-
izations may qualify for special terms when ordering
quantities of this title. For information, write Special Sales
Department, Newmarket Press, 18 East 48th Street, New
York, NY 10017; call (212) 832-3575; fax (212) 832-3629;
or e-mail mailbox@newmarketpress.com.

www.newmarketpress.com

Design by Timothy Shaner.

Manufactured in the United States of America.

Other Newmarket Pictorial Moviebooks include:
*Gods and Generals: The Illustrated Story
of the Epic Civil War Film*
Chicago: The Movie and Lyrics
Catch Me If You Can: The Film and the Filmmakers
Frida: Bringing Frida Kahlo's Life and Art to Film
*E.T. The Extra-Terrestrial from Concept to Classic: The
Illustrated Story of the Film and the Filmmakers*
*Windtalkers: The Making of the Film about the Navajo Code
Talkers of World War II*
Ali: The Movie and the Man
Planet of the Apes: Re-imagined by Tim Burton
*Moulin Rouge: The Splendid Book That Charts
the Journey of Baz Luhrmann's Motion Picture*
The Art of The Matrix
Gladiator: The Making of the Ridley Scott Epic
*Crouching Tiger, Hidden Dragon:
A Portrait of the Ang Lee Film*
*Titus: The Illustrated Screenplay, Adapted
from the Play by William Shakespeare*
*The Age of Innocence: A Portrait of the Film
Based on the Novel by Edith Wharton*
Cradle Will Rock: The Movie and the Moment
Saving Private Ryan: The Men, the Mission, the Movie

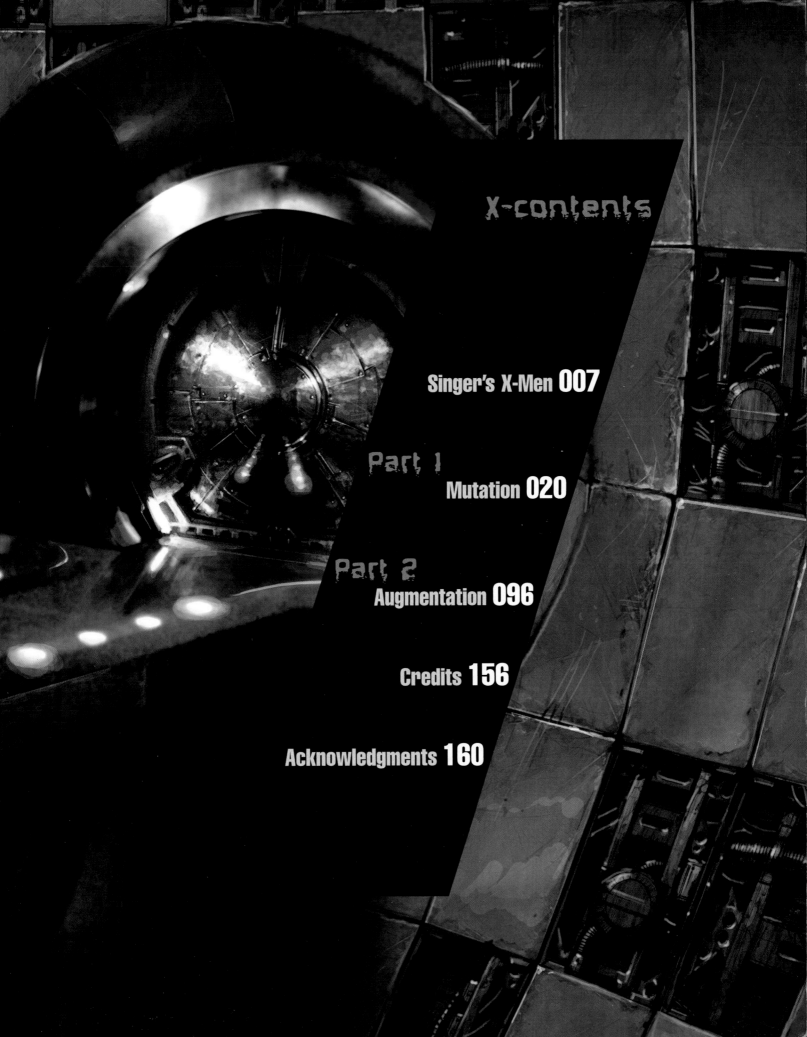

X-contents

On the first

weekend of August 2002, Bryan Singer flew from the Vancouver, British Columbia, set of *X-Men 2*, to San Diego, California, for Comicon, the world's largest comic book convention. *X-Men*, released two summers earlier, had more than won over the proud devotees of *X-Men* comics, alleviating their pre-release angst about how their favorite heroes would be rendered on the big screen. For Singer, it was a rare public appearance and a personally important journey. "As much as I believe our X-Men films will play to a wider audience and will be entertaining, the fans of the comic book are the core audience and their interest and their fan-ship is something I never take for granted for a moment," says Singer. "Some people have followed this universe for 40 years—to not make a film that inspires them or to not take them seriously, what would be the point? Then what are you making the movie for? Money? I have never made a picture to make money."

Despite Singer's pure motives, in 2000 the faithful and the uninitiated together embraced *X-Men* and propelled it to the second-biggest opening of any film in Twentieth Century Fox history (exceeded only by *Star Wars: Episode 1*), going on to earn close to $300 million at the worldwide box office. Moreover, the film could lay claim to leading the resurgence of comic books adapted for the big screen featuring A-list actors and directors, laying the groundwork for such films as *Spider-Man* in 2002 and Ang Lee's *The Hulk* in 2003.

Even with the knowledge that he was welcome with this crowd, Singer was floored by the reception his appearance at Comicon 2002 generated. Some 1,000 fans had turned up to see him at the same conference two years earlier, but this time five times as many were jammed into a massive ballroom, which Singer entered to thunderous applause.

It was clear that expectations were running high, and once again Singer did not want to disappoint. He had cobbled together an early trailer of the new film—no easy feat considering he was only three weeks into shooting and none of the special effects (F/X) were yet in place. What was in place, however, were the accomplished ensemble of principal actors including Patrick Stewart (Professor Xavier), Hugh Jackman (Wolverine), Sir Ian McKellen (Magneto), Halle Berry (Storm), Famke Janssen (Jean Grey), James Marsden (Cyclops), Anna Paquin (Rogue), Rebecca Romijn-Stamos (Mystique), Bruce Davison (Senator Kelly), and Shawn Ashmore (Iceman).

The trailer rolled and the image of Stewart's Professor

LEFT: Director Bryan Singer on the Plastic Prison set. RIGHT: X-ray illustration created by Guy H. Dyas as set dressing for the augmentation room's X-ray wall. PREVIOUS PAGES: Concept illustration of Dark Cerebro by Mark Goerner.

Xavier and McKellen's Magneto exchanging ominous words over a translucent plastic chess board flashed on a screen. When the trailer finished, the auditorium was on its feet and the count-down to the much-anticipated movie was in full flight. Now, all Singer had to do was fly back to Canada, where the film was in production, and get it done.

Of course the success of the first movie assured that there would be a sequel—with most of the original creative and production team staying on—but it also gave Singer an opportunity to stretch his directorial and story-telling legs. "There's nothing like a successful movie to breed a bigger sequel," notes Avi Arad, the head of Marvel Studios, the film arm of the comic book company from which the X-Men franchise is adapted, and an executive producer of the movie. "It's bigger in scope and better, and it introduces new characters in an interesting way." For Singer, "bigger" is a word that comes up again and again when discussing his vision for *X2*. Certainly there would be more special effects this second time around (partly reflecting a considerably bigger production budget for the second film), resulting in some 800 on-screen F/X sequence versus 500 in *X-Men*. "With this one," says Singer, "I could have more fun with the characters and make a slightly deeper, bigger, funnier and more romantic movie." Perhaps *Los Angeles Times* film critic Kenneth Turan laid the foundation best for what was to come in his July 2000 review of *X-Men*. "There are 10 mutants, each with a different superpower to introduce, a plot to unfold, jokes to make, visuals complex enough to employ more than a dozen effects houses to display and enough action to keep 60 stunt people occupied," wrote Turan. "So much is happening you feel the immediate need of a sequel just as a reward for absorbing it all."

That "reward" was certainly built into Singer's thinking when he co-wrote the initial story for *X-Men* with executive producer Tom DeSanto. It was DeSanto, a long-time comic book fan, who brought Singer into the world of the X-Men. "Bryan had never read comics so his initial reaction about doing a comic book film was less than enthusiastic, but after many a conversation I won him over with the analogy of *X-Men* being Malcolm X (Magneto), Martin Luther King (Xavier), and the next

wave in human evolution. Now he is one of the biggest champions of the mythology," says DeSanto. The first installment introduced Xavier's "good" mutants allied against "bad" mutants led by the powerful Magneto, and a couple of intriguing storylines—one about the government lawmakers persecuting mutants and the other about the murky Canadian origins of Wolverine, whose powers couple the mysterious ability to quickly heal from wounds with a skeleton and retractable claws made of an impossibly strong alloy.

Both of these themes set the stage for what came in *X2:* A brazen attack on the President of the United States by a new, powerful mutant character—Nightcrawler—fuels the political and public outcry for a Mutant Registration Act and an anti-mutant movement led by the spooky William Stryker (played by Brian Cox), a former Army commander who may also hold the key to Wolverine's, A.K.A. Logan's, origins. Stryker launches a bold offensive on Xavier's mansion fortress, leading to a new mutant alliance between Xavier's X-Men and their foe Magneto against their common enemy.

"X-*Men* introduced a complex universe of characters and a sense of pending conflict," says Singer. "The first movie introduced the X-Men lore to a new audience and established the conflicting philosophies embodied by Professor Xavier and Magneto. Professor Xavier's goal is peaceful co-existence between humans and mutants. While, on the other hand, Magneto believes in mutant supremacy. In *X2*, the conflict is taken to the next level, where the future of mutant and humankind are in jeopardy."

"There were many different characters and storylines that we wished to pursue and interweave within this second install-ment," recalls producer Lauren Shuler Donner. "We wanted to go further with the characterization," adds producer Ralph Winter, "and one of the approaches we took was to explore Logan's origins."

With the basic story outline in hand, the filmmakers turned their attentions to adding characters familiar to comics fans but new to the film franchise. In unfolding the "X-Universe," Singer

LEFT: Producer Ralph Winter (left), Bryan Singer, and co-producer Ross Fanger (right) between takes on the White House set. ABOVE LEFT: Shooting a scene on the Oval Office set. ABOVE RIGHT: Producer Lauren Shuler Donner has a conversation with Hugh Jackman. BACKGROUND: Alkali Dam illustration by Mark Goerner.

X2.009

also wanted to make sure that different generations of mutants were portrayed—from infants to seniors. Discussions were held as to which major new character would end up in the film: Gambit, Beast, or Nightcrawler. The nod went to Nightcrawler, perhaps the most outcast of all the X-Men—a figure ridiculed by society and made to feel a freak until he ended up in a circus. The filmmakers saw the character as a symbol of intolerance, one of the key themes of the comics and the movies. "He, in his own way, represents the mutant conflict," says Singer. "He is a deeply religious character who has the physical appearance of a demon. He has this unique power of teleporting [known on the *X-Men* set as "Bamf-ing" in tribute to the "Bamf" that appears in a smoke cloud in the comics every time the character teleports]. He can be very dangerous but at the same time he's also kind of whimsical."

In casting Nightcrawler, the filmmakers looked for an actor who had uniqueness and comic timing, qualities long established for the character in the comics. "Alan Cumming has that extra sense of comic timing and comic inventiveness," says Shuler Donner. "His essence is fascinating. If you're in a room with Alan, your eyes go right to him. That works for the character. We needed Nightcrawler to draw you in not by his blue make-up, but by what's underneath the blue make-up, his versatility, his believability and his vulnerability."

Also new to the X-Men motion picture universe is Pyro, played by Aaron Stanford. The filmmakers were looking to include a character who wanted to be part of the X-Men, but whose powers ultimately would overcome the X-Men philosophy. Another new addition is Lady Deathstrike, a character as low-key and understated as her name would suggest. Played with beautiful menace by Kelly Hu, Deathstrike is essentially a female Wolverine, except she is definitely not on the good guys' side. "I have only one line in the entire film," notes Hu, admitting that at first she was initially unhappy about this. "Then I was assured that Rebecca Romijn-Stamos (Mystique) also had only one line in *X-Men*, and she was one of the most memorable characters in the whole film."

Indeed, one of *X2*'s signature scenes is the battle

OPPOSITE: Filming a scene with Famke Janssen. ABOVE: Green screen shot of Dark Cerebro. LEFT: Halle Berry on the X-Jet set.

between Deathstrike and Wolverine. It was conceived as one of the most searing and terrifying fights imaginable, since both assailants possess not only the power to shred victims with their claws but also to heal themselves rapidly. "They didn't want it to look kung-fuey and martial-artsy," says Hu. "They just wanted them to be vicious and mean."

The scene played to one of Singer's favorite aspects of the X-Men's world, that its characters' powers—or rather, "mutations"—tend to be quite elaborate and even opaque compared to a typical super-hero's power of speed, super-strength, flight, or x-ray vision. X-Men do complex things like control metal, change shapes or emit strange forms of energy—all of which present unique challenges and new possibilities for presenting them on film. In one of the film's subversively humorous moments, while the super-sleek X-Jet packed full of mutants is being pursued by Air Force F-16s, a frustrated Wolverine yells out: "Aren't there any weapons in this heap?" Of course it is only moments before he realizes the weapons are belted into their seats and include himself.

Behind the scenes—literally—one significant new addition to the *X-Men* team was production designer Guy Hendrix Dyas who had mostly worked as an illustrator and had never before overseen a movie. He had done conceptual design work on such films as *Pearl Harbor* and the *The Cell* and got to know Singer through their initial work on a revival of the TV series *Battlestar Galactica* (which had to be halted when *X2* geared up). DeSanto recalls, "We worked with Guy on *Galactica* for about eight months and Guy has this tremendous gift of respecting the mythology, but also seeing beyond it and creating a vision of what it could be." Singer enlisted Dyas to do some early sketches for *X2*, and then hired him to build on the template created by production designer John Myhre in *X-Men*. "I was so impressed by his energy and his style," Singer recalls. "It was both reverential to John Myhre's original designs but then took it beyond it to the next level."

Although the original *X-Men* was filmed in Toronto, the production elected to film the new film across Canada, in Vancouver, in part because it was closer to Los Angeles.

Filming began on location in Victoria, the provincial capital

ABOVE: Bryan Singer directs actor Ian McKellen. ABOVE LEFT: Production designer Guy H. Dyas in the Vancouver, B.C. production office. BACKGROUND: Entrance to Stryker's Control Room. Illustration by Mark Goerner.

X2.013

014.X2

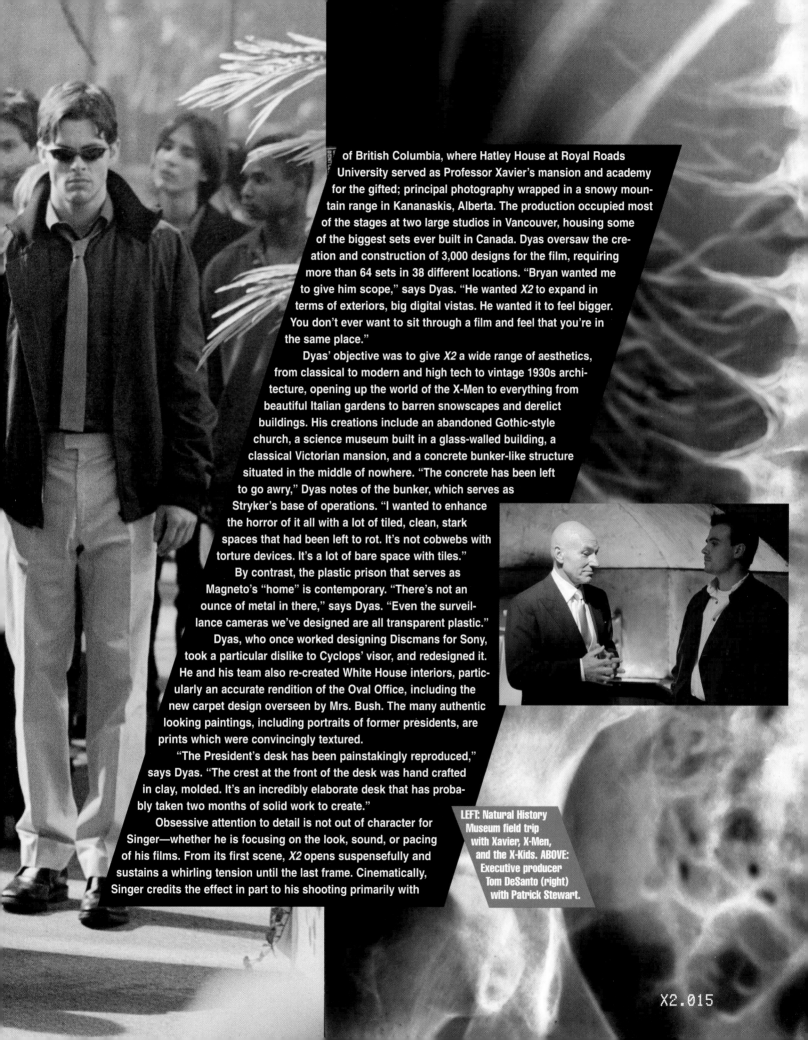

of British Columbia, where Hatley House at Royal Roads University served as Professor Xavier's mansion and academy for the gifted; principal photography wrapped in a snowy mountain range in Kananaskis, Alberta. The production occupied most of the stages at two large studios in Vancouver, housing some of the biggest sets ever built in Canada. Dyas oversaw the creation and construction of 3,000 designs for the film, requiring more than 64 sets in 38 different locations. "Bryan wanted me to give him scope," says Dyas. "He wanted *X2* to expand in terms of exteriors, big digital vistas. He wanted it to feel bigger. You don't ever want to sit through a film and feel that you're in the same place."

Dyas' objective was to give *X2* a wide range of aesthetics, from classical to modern and high tech to vintage 1930s architecture, opening up the world of the X-Men to everything from beautiful Italian gardens to barren snowscapes and derelict buildings. His creations include an abandoned Gothic-style church, a science museum built in a glass-walled building, a classical Victorian mansion, and a concrete bunker-like structure situated in the middle of nowhere. "The concrete has been left to go awry," Dyas notes of the bunker, which serves as Stryker's base of operations. "I wanted to enhance the horror of it all with a lot of tiled, clean, stark spaces that had been left to rot. It's not cobwebs with torture devices. It's a lot of bare space with tiles."

By contrast, the plastic prison that serves as Magneto's "home" is contemporary. "There's not an ounce of metal in there," says Dyas. "Even the surveillance cameras we've designed are all transparent plastic." Dyas, who once worked designing Discmans for Sony, took a particular dislike to Cyclops' visor, and redesigned it. He and his team also re-created White House interiors, particularly an accurate rendition of the Oval Office, including the new carpet design overseen by Mrs. Bush. The many authentic looking paintings, including portraits of former presidents, are prints which were convincingly textured.

"The President's desk has been painstakingly reproduced," says Dyas. "The crest at the front of the desk was hand crafted in clay, molded. It's an incredibly elaborate desk that has probably taken two months of solid work to create."

Obsessive attention to detail is not out of character for Singer—whether he is focusing on the look, sound, or pacing of his films. From its first scene, *X2* opens suspensefully and sustains a whirling tension until the last frame. Cinematically, Singer credits the effect in part to his shooting primarily with

LEFT: Natural History Museum field trip with Xavier, X-Men, and the X-Kids. ABOVE: Executive producer Tom DeSanto (right) with Patrick Stewart.

super 35mm film using spherical lenses rather than the anamorphic cameras he relied on for *X-Men*. The advantages of super 35mm include being more flexible, requiring less time to set up between takes, which helps keep the flow going among the actors and crew. "Shooting in anamorphic was a pleasure to do. But ultimately I find myself able to shoot quicker and with more flexibility and with lower light conditions with super 35 with spherical lenses," says Singer. "It was one of many things that made my life a lot easier this time around." Indeed, as actress Famke Jannsen (Jean Grey) puts it: "The good thing about it was that we all knew each other and we knew Brian and his approach to filmmaking."

In the *X-Men* stories, Professor Charles Xavier is the headmaster of his school for the gifted. It's hard not to draw the parallel that Singer is to his talented ensemble and crew what Xavier is to his mutants. Upstairs from the movie's post-production editing rooms in Hollywood, Singer occupied a big, old, and very spare office distinguished only by a few cool pieces of X-Men art, including a bronze bust of Wolverine on his conference table, a model X-Jet on his desk and some classic scenes of Professor X from the original 1960s comic blown up and framed on the walls. When he was hired to do *X-Men*, Singer was a 32-year-old cinema whiz from New Jersey who had never read comic books or directed an action movie. But putting together an ensemble of accomplished stars and relative newcomers played to his strengths. He had instantly established himself as a virtuoso of dark suspense and ensemble-cast cinema with his 1995 debut hit *The Usual Suspects*. "In X-Men movies, we decided to have real actors—terrific actors—and use visual effects as a support tool," he explains. "These are character-driven movies with some of this spectacle in it." Singer is also a longtime *Star Trek* fan who understood the challenges—and responsibility—of bringing beloved characters and stories to life. (As a Trekker, working with Patrick Stewart—Trek-world's noble Captain Picard—was a thrill in and of itself for Singer, and it also gained him a cameo as a crewman on the bridge of the Enterprise in the recent *Star Trek: Nemesis*. An even bigger thrill? One night, Stewart and his wife invited Singer over to his Los Angeles home for dinner. The doorbell rang, and standing there was none other than Captain Kirk himself, William Shatner. "The most unbelievable thing," recalls

ABOVE RIGHT: (from left to right) screenwriter Mike Dougherty, *X-Men* creator Stan Lee, screenwriter Dan Harris, and associate producer David Gorder. ABOVE: Visual effects supervisor Michael Fink (left) with co-editor Elliot Graham. BACKGROUND: Wolverine enters the abandoned base in search of his past. Concept illustration by Guy H. Dyas.

KELLY HU
"YURIKO"

BRIAN COX
"WILLIAM STRYKER"

REBECCA
ROMIJN-STAMOS
"MYSTIQUE"

IAN McKELLEN

018.X2

Singer, "was playing *Next-Generation* pinball with Shatner in Patrick Stewart's den.")

An only child who was adopted, Singer grew up in Princeton Junction, New Jersey, where his mother was an environmental activist and his father was credit manager for Maidenform, the women's undergarments company. His high school friends included actor Ethan Hawke and screenwriters Chris McQuarrie (who wrote the script for *The Usual Suspects*) and Brandon Boyce (who wrote Singer's second major film, *Apt Pupil*). Singer used Hawke to make an 8mm film called *Lion's Den*, while attending film school at USC. In his last semester, a Japanese financier gave Singer $250,000 to produce *Public Access*, a film written by McQuarrie and co-starring Boyce that won the coveted Grand Jury Prize at the 1993 Sundance Film Festival. That acclaim led to Singer developing and directing the stylishly intricate *The Usual Suspects*, which earned two Oscars. He followed that up with *Apt Pupil*, based on a Stephen King novella that Singer read when he was 19 and optioned for $1 with a friend from USC based on a screenplay Singer and Boyce developed. Singer once told the *Los Angeles Times* that years ago, before the studios came to him, he worked security at a black-tie event in Hollywood and nervously introduced him-self to Stephen Spielberg. After *The Usual Suspects*, Spielberg invited him to his office and they struck up a friend-ship. Spielberg, along with Robert Altman, ended up sponsoring Singer's membership in the Directors Guild of America.

After the success of *The Usual Suspects*, Singer also met and befriended Stan Lee, who along with artist Jack Kirby had created *X-Men* for Marvel.

All of these achievements have of course put Singer in a rarified realm among directors, at a rela-tively tender age. Even still, as his humbling appearance at Comicon reminded him, *X-Men* is one of those rare cultural totems that can transcend moviemaking. Like the imaginary Professor Xavier, it seems Singer was mustering all his forces—both human and mutant—to take the world of the X-Men to the next level.

ABOVE: 12 cast members and Bryan Singer assembled for a Vancouver press conference, 2002. RIGHT: Bryan Singer on set in the Alberta wilderness. Photos by Dan Harris. BACK-GROUND: Illustration by Mark Goerner

Part 1
Mutation

MUTANTS. SINCE THE DISCOVERY OF THEIR

EXISTENCE, THEY HAVE BEEN REGARDED WITH

FEAR, SUSPICION, AND OFTEN HATRED. ACROSS

THE PLANET, DEBATE RAGES: ARE MUTANTS THE

NEXT LINK IN THE EVOLUTIONARY CHAIN...

OR SIMPLY A NEW SPECIES OF HUMANITY,

FIGHTING FOR THEIR SHARE OF THE WORLD?

EITHER WAY, ONE FACT HAS BEEN HISTORICALLY

PROVEN: SHARING THE WORLD HAS NEVER BEEN

HUMANITY'S DEFINING ATTRIBUTE.

Nightcrawler disguises himself as one of the members of a tour group to enter the White House. To cover the unusual blue color of his skin he wears a long raincoat, a hat, sunglasses, and applies white make-up (a trick he kept from his days as a circus performer) to cover his face and neck. Later on, during Nightcrawler's actual attack on the president, his disguise comes off to reveal his true features for the first time.

ABOVE and RIGHT: Alan Cumming as Nightcrawler. RIGHT INSET: Costume illustration by James Oxford, for costume designer Louise Mingenbach.

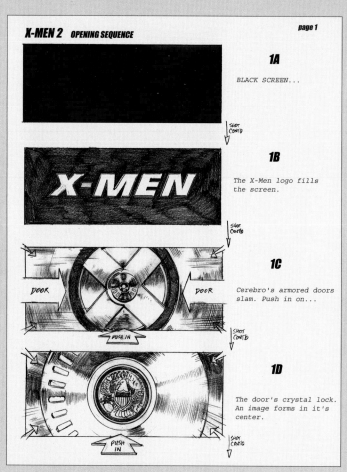

1A

BLACK SCREEN...

1B

The X-Men logo fills the screen.

1C

Cerebro's armored doors slam. Push in on...

DOOR DOOR

PUSH IN

1D

The door's crystal lock. An image forms in it's center.

PUSH IN

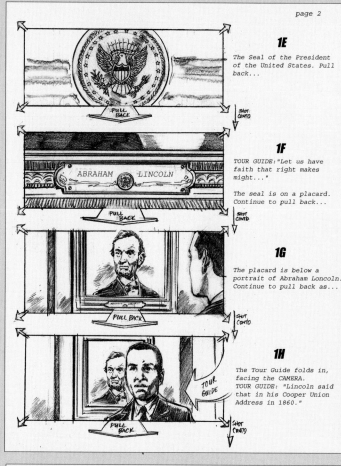

1E

The Seal of the President of the United States. Pull back...

PULL BACK

1F

ABRAHAM · LINCOLN

TOUR GUIDE:"Let us have faith that right makes might..."

The seal is on a placard. Continue to pull back...

PULL BACK

1G

The placard is below a portrait of Abraham Loncoln. Continue to pull back as...

PULL BACK

1H

The Tour Guide folds in, facing the CAMERA.
TOUR GUIDE: "Lincoln said that in his Cooper Union Address in 1860."

TOUR GUIDE

PULL BACK

1J

Continue to pull back to reveal the tour group.

PULL BACK

CUT

2

Wide. The tour group in the Entrance Hall of the White House.

CUT

3

Track past faces in the crowd. In the b.g. we see a whisp of smoke coming from behind a pilar.

TRACK

CUT

4A

Track through the crowd...

TRACK

4B

NC ENTERS

...to a lone man wearing a baseball cap.

TRACK

CUT

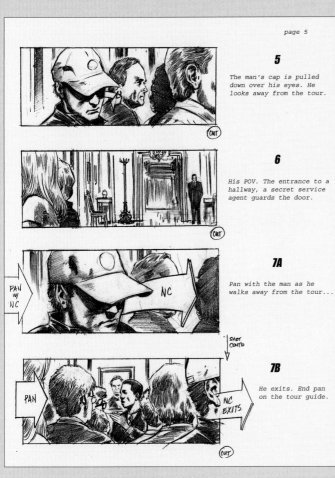

5

The man's cap is pulled down over his eyes. He looks away from the tour.

CUT

6

His POV. The entrance to a hallway, a secret service agent guards the door.

CUT

7A

PAN w/ NC

NC

Pan with the man as he walks away from the tour...

SHOT CONT'D

7B

PAN

NC EXITS

He exits. End pan on the tour guide.

CUT

8A

NC

CAMERA W/ NC

CAMERA follows the man toward the hall...

SHOT CONT'D

8B

AGENT

The secret service agent blocks his way.
AGENT #1:"Can I help you?"

CUT

9

Angle over the agent on the man. He doesn't answer.

CUT

10

Angle over the Man on the Agent.
AGENT #1:"You alright, sir? Are you lost?"

CUT

11A

The man looks up...

SHOT CONT'D

11B

Revealing his face. It's the face of a demon. Yhis is Kurt Wagner - aka Nightcrawler.
"Yes...I'm lost."

CUT

12A

Angle behind Nightcrawler. Pull back as...

TAIL

PULL BACK

SHOT CONT'D

12B

...a prehensile tail snakes out from under his coat.

CUT

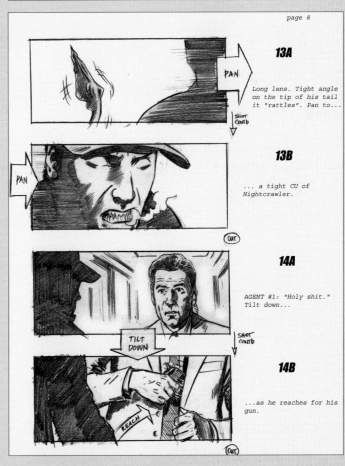

13A

PAN

Long lens. Tight angle on the tip of his tail it "rattles". Pan to...

SHOT CONT'D

13B

PAN

... a tight CU of Nightcrawler.

CUT

14A

AGENT #1: "Holy shit."
Tilt down...

TILT DOWN

SHOT CONT'D

14B

REACH

...as he reaches for his gun.

CUT

Artist: Gabriel Hardman

X2.027

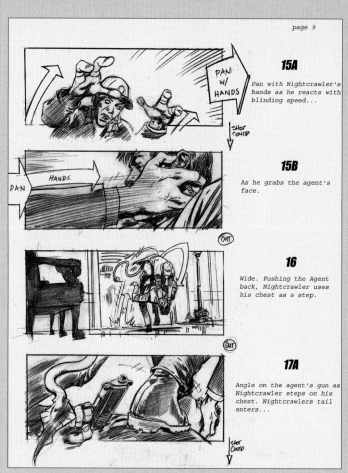

15A

Pan with Nightcrawler's hands as he reacts with blinding speed...

15B

As he grabs the agent's face.

16

Wide. Pushing the Agent back, Nightcrawler uses his chest as a step.

17A

Angle on the agent's gun as Nightcrawler steps on his chest. Nightcrawlers tail enters...

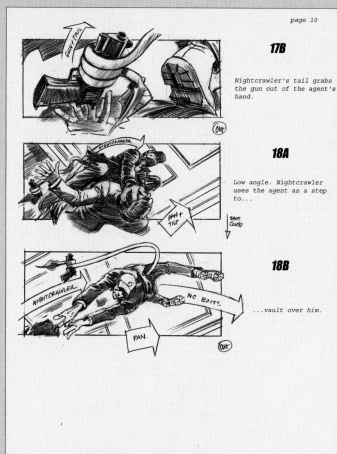

17B

Nightcrawler's tail grabs the gun out of the agent's hand.

18A

Low angle. Nightcrawler uses the agent as a step to...

18B

...vault over him.

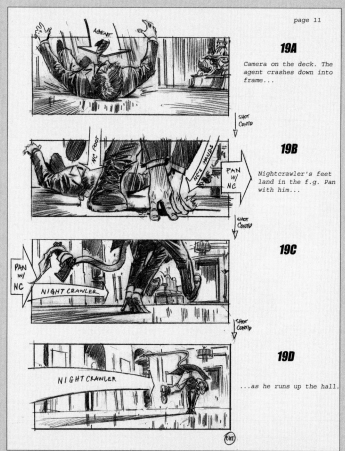

19A

Camera on the deck. The agent crashes down into frame...

19B

Nightcrawler's feet land in the f.g. Pan with him...

19C

19D

...as he runs up the hall.

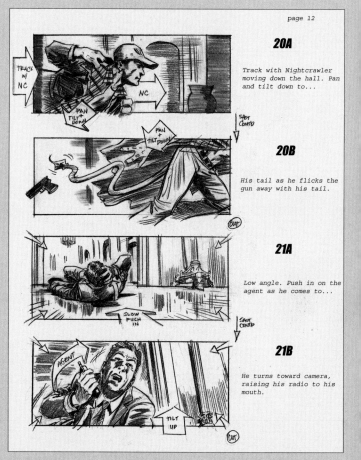

20A

Track with Nightcrawler moving down the hall. Pan and tilt down to...

20B

His tail as he flicks the gun away with his tail.

21A

Low angle. Push in on the agent as he comes to...

21B

He turns toward camera, raising his radio to his mouth.

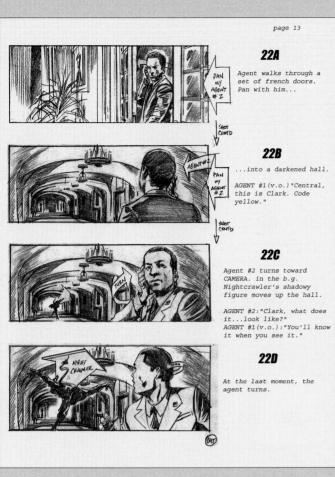

22A

PAN W/ AGENT #2

Agent walks through a set of french doors. Pan with him...

SHOT CONT'D

22B

AGENT #1

PAN W/ AGENT #2

...into a darkened hall.

AGENT #1 (v.o.): "Central, this is Clark. Code yellow."

SHOT CONT'D

22C

TURN

Agent #2 turns toward CAMERA. in the b.g. Nightcrawler's shadowy figure moves up the hall.

AGENT #2: "Clark, what does it...look like?"
AGENT #1 (v.o.): "You'll know it when you see it."

22D

NIGHTCRAWLER

At the last moment, the agent turns.

CUT

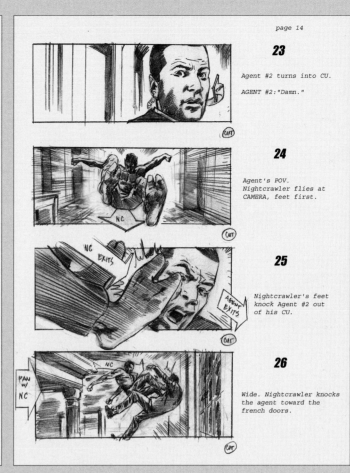

23

TURN

Agent #2 turns into CU.

AGENT #2: "Damn."

CUT

24

NC

Agent's POV. Nightcrawler flies at CAMERA, feet first.

CUT

25

NC EXITS

AGENT EXITS

Nightcrawler's feet knock Agent #2 out of his CU.

CUT

26

PAN W/ NC

NC

Wide. Nightcrawler knocks the agent toward the french doors.

CUT

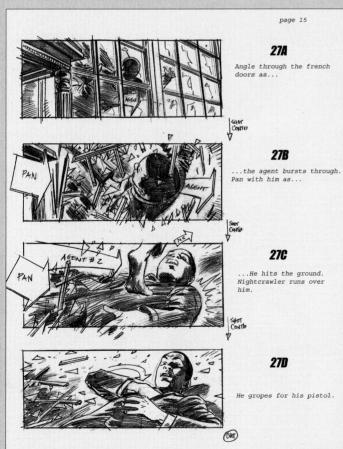

27A

AGENT

Angle through the french doors as...

SHOT CONT'D

27B

PAN

AGENT

...the agent bursts through. Pan with him as...

SHOT CONT'D

27C

PAN

AGENT #2

NC

...He hits the ground. Nightcrawler runs over him.

SHOT CONT'D

27D

He gropes for his pistol.

CUT

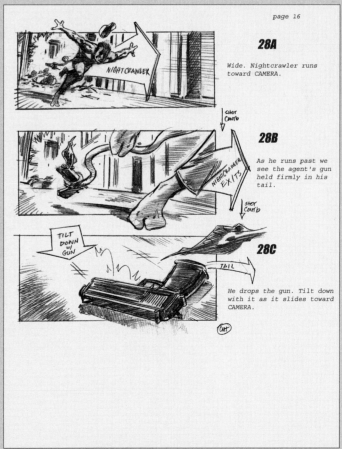

28A

NIGHTCRAWLER

Wide. Nightcrawler runs toward CAMERA.

SHOT CONT'D

28B

NIGHTCRAWLER EXITS

As he runs past we see the agent's gun held firmly in his tail.

SHOT CONT'D

28C

TILT DOWN W/ GUN

TAIL

He drops the gun. Tilt down with it as it slides toward CAMERA.

CUT

Artist: Gabriel Hardman

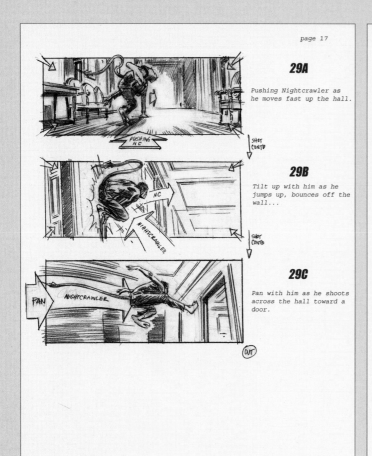

29A

Pushing Nightcrawler as he moves fast up the hall.

29B

Tilt up with him as he jumps up, bounces off the wall...

29C

Pan with him as he shoots across the hall toward a door.

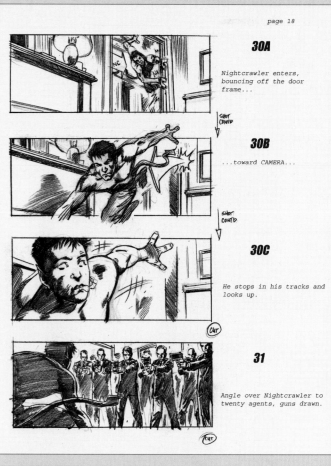

30A

Nightcrawler enters, bouncing off the door frame...

30B

...toward CAMERA...

30C

He stops in his tracks and looks up.

31

Angle over Nightcrawler to twenty agents, guns drawn.

32A

Resume angle on Nightcrawler. More agents run through the door he entered.

32B

He turns as they pull their guns.

32C

Pan with Nightcrawler as he turns.

33

Nightcrawler's POV. Five more agents rush in the opposite door.

34

Push in on Nightcrawler.

NIGHTCRAWLER: "Verdammt."

35

LEAD AGENT: "DOWN ON THE GROUND NOW! DO IT NOW!"

36A

Angle past the agents to Nightcrawler. Boom down w/ him as...

36B

...he slowly gets down on the floor.

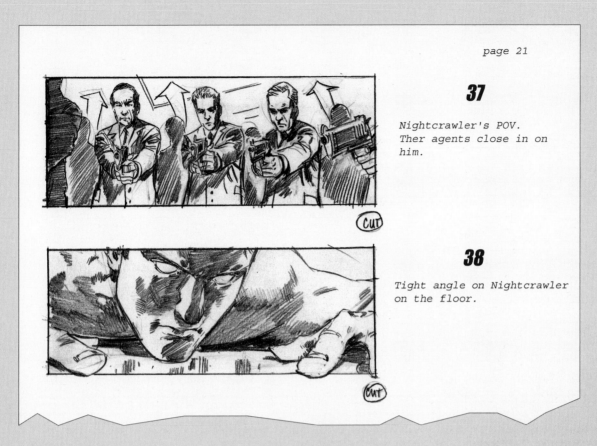

page 21

37

*Nightcrawler's POV.
Ther agents close in on
him.*

CUT

38

*Tight angle on Nightcrawler
on the floor.*

CUT

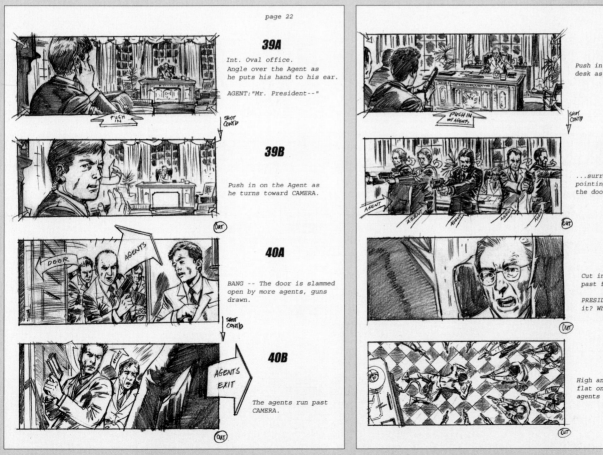

page 22

39A

Int. Oval office.
Angle over the Agent as
he puts his hand to his ear.

AGENT:"Mr. President--"

PUSH IN

SHOT CONT'D

39B

Push in on the Agent as
he turns toward CAMERA.

CUT

40A

DOOR

AGENTS

BANG -- The door is slammed
open by more agents, guns
drawn.

SHOT CONT'D

40B

AGENTS EXIT

The agents run past
CAMERA.

CUT

page 23

41A

Push in on the president's
desk as the agents...

PUSH IN W/AGENTS

SHOT CONT'D

41B

AGENT ACENT AGENT AGENT AGENT

...surround the desk,
pointing their guns at
the doors.

CUT

42

Cut in on the president
past f.g. agents.

PRESIDENT WILKES: "What is
it? What's happening?"

CUT

43

High angle over Nightcrawler,
flat on the floor. The
agents close in on him.

CUT

Artist: Gabriel Hardman

X2.031

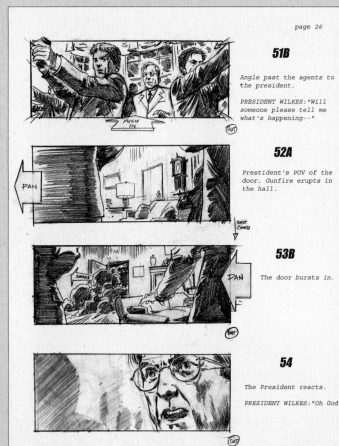

44

Angle on two other agents.

AGENT #3 LEWIS: "Who gives a -- Kill it before it gets up."

45

Angle on Nightcrawler on the ground.

46

LEAD AGENT: "Shut up, Lewis. You're not going to give us any trouble, are you pal?"

47

Nightcrawler smiles.

48

Lewis fires.

49

Angle over the agents as Nightcrawler explodes in a burst of black smoke.

50

The Agents react.

51A

INT. OVAL OFFICE. The agents surround the president.

51B

Angle past the agents to the president.

PRESIDENT WILKES: "Will someone please tell me what's happening--"

52A

President's POV of the door. Gunfire erupts in the hall.

53B

The door bursts in.

54

The President reacts.

PRESIDENT WILKES: "Oh God.

54A

The room fills with smoke, men and guns.

54B

The lead agent sees the President.

LEAD AGENT: "Get him out of here!"

Whip pan to:

54C

The agents in front of the president.
OVAL OFFICE AGENT: "Where's our bogey?"

55

LEAD AGENT: "I don't know."

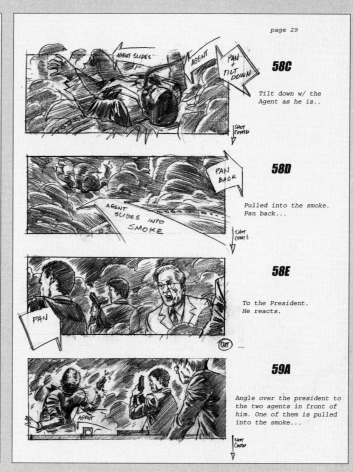

56

High Angle over the president, Agents circle him. They stand on the presidential seal. Smoke fills the room.

57

The president is enveloped in smoke.

58A

Angle on one of the Agents in the circle as...

58B

His feet are pulled out from under him. Pan and tilt w/ him...

58C

Tilt down w/ the Agent as he is..

58D

Pulled into the smoke. Pan back...

58E

To the President. He reacts.

59A

Angle over the president to the two agents in front of him. One of them is pulled into the smoke...

59B

Then the other is pulled into the smoke.

60A

Wilkes reacts.

60B

The Lead Agent steps into the f.g., in front of the President.

61

Lead Agent's POV. Pan across the smoke filled room.

62A

Tight angle on the Lead Agent as he looks around...

62B

...then looks up.

63A

Low angle past the Lead Agent as...

63B

...Nightcrawler's face bursts out of the smoke above him.

Artist: Gabriel Hardman

64

Tight angle over Nightcrawler on the Lead Agent. He reacts.

65A

Cut to Wilkes. He reacts. Nightcrawler's tail shoots down into frame...

65B

Then Wraps around Wilkes neck...

65C

Lifting him up out of frame.

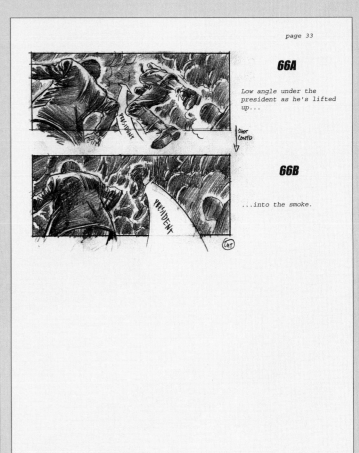

66A

Low angle under the president as he's lifted up...

66B

...into the smoke.

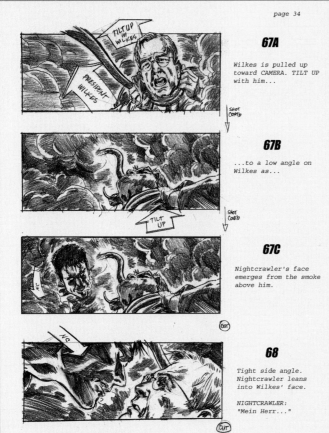

67A

Wilkes is pulled up toward CAMERA. TILT UP with him...

67B

...to a low angle on Wilkes as...

67C

Nightcrawler's face emerges from the smoke above him.

68

Tight side angle. Nightcrawler leans into Wilkes' face.

NIGHTCRAWLER:
"Mein Herr..."

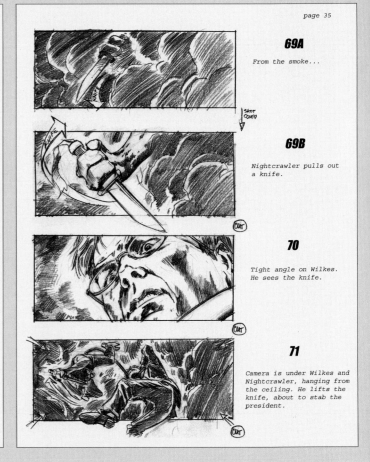

69A

From the smoke...

69B

Nightcrawler pulls out a knife.

70

Tight angle on Wilkes. He sees the knife.

71

Camera is under Wilkes and Nightcrawler, hanging from the ceiling. He lifts the knife, about to stab the president.

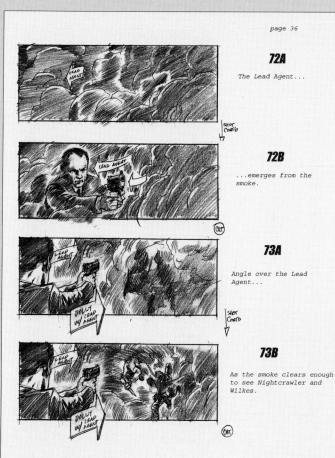

page 36

72A

The Lead Agent...

72B

...emerges from the smoke.

73A

Angle over the Lead Agent...

73B

As the smoke clears enough to see Nightcrawler and Wilkes.

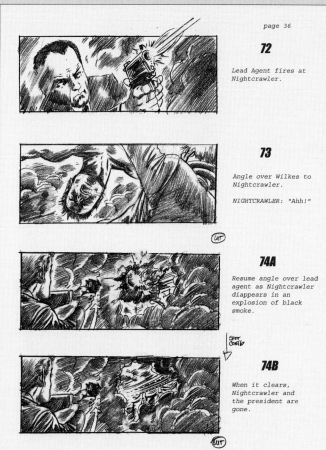

page 36

72

Lead Agent fires at Nightcrawler.

73

Angle over Wilkes to Nightcrawler.

NIGHTCRAWLER: "Ahh!"

74A

Resume angle over lead agent as Nightcrawler diappears in an explosion of black smoke.

74B

When it clears, Nightcrawler and the president are gone.

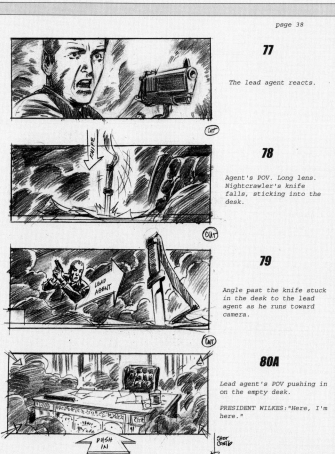

psge 38

77

The lead agent reacts.

78

Agent's POV. Long lens. Nightcrawler's knife falls, sticking into the desk.

79

Angle past the knife stuck in the desk to the lead agent as he runs toward camera.

80A

Lead agent's POV pushing in on the empty desk.

PRESIDENT WILKES:"Here, I'm here."

page 39

80B

Agent's POV cont'd. Push past the desk to reveal Wilkes on the floor where he fell when Nightcrawler teleported.

81

Angle past Wilkes to the lead agent as he comes around the desk.

82

The lead agent and Wilkes look back at the desk.

83

Push in on the knife sticking in the desk top. The ribbon reads "MUTANT FREEDOM NOW".

Artist: Gabriel Hardman

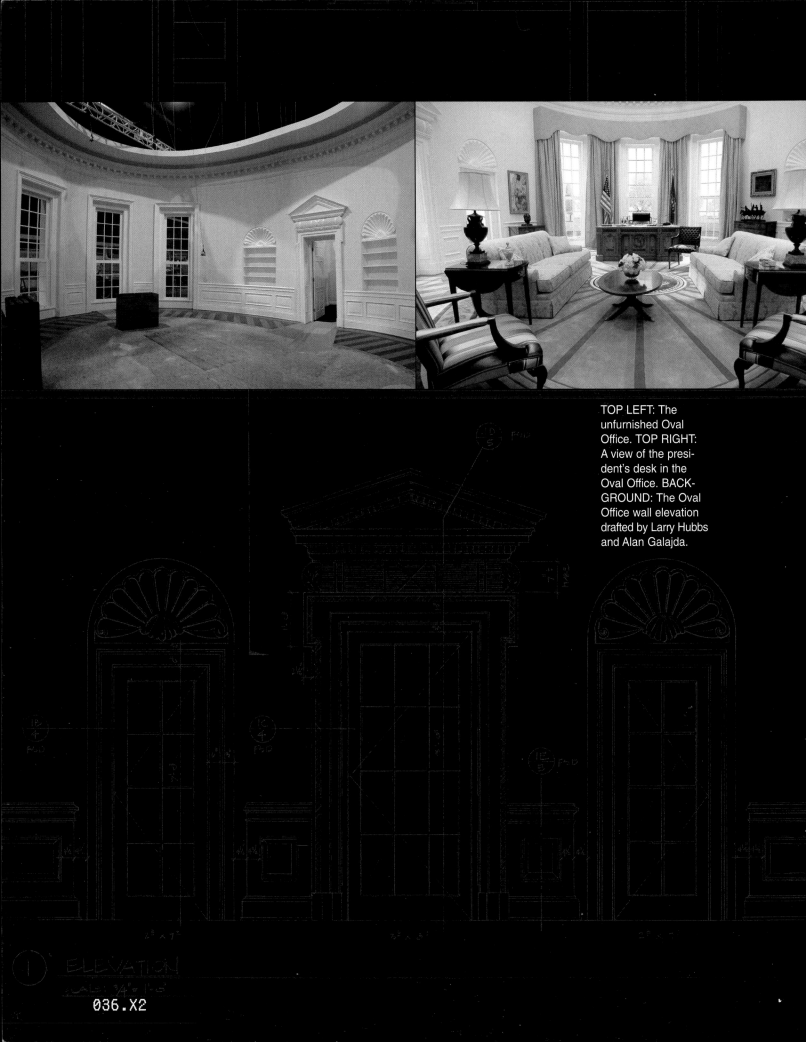

TOP LEFT: The unfurnished Oval Office. TOP RIGHT: A view of the president's desk in the Oval Office. BACKGROUND: The Oval Office wall elevation drafted by Larry Hubbs and Alan Galajda.

ELEVATION

036.X2

Although the Oval Office was built as an exact replica both in size and in furnishings, the rest of the White House is a condensed version designed to accommodate the elaborate nature of Nightcrawler's acrobatics and stunts. The corridors are slightly larger in scale, providing more fighting room, and many fixtures (including the picture frames) were made of rubber for safety reasons.

RIGHT: The White House set in mid-construction.
BELOW: An overview of the finished Oval Office set. Photos by Guy H. Dyas.

Pre-production costume and character illustrations for the Nightcrawler character by James Oxford. RIGHT: Special effects make-up designer Gordon Smith oversees the application of the special blue body paint needed to complete Nightcrawler's look on test subject Matt Granger.

X2.039

ABOVE: An illustration by Jean-François Mignault, depicting Nightcrawler's characteristic hands. This art was created as a guide for the make-up FX department to build the final prosthetics worn by Alan Cumming in the film. RIGHT: Gordon Smith wearing Nightcrawler's tail. FAR RIGHT: James Oxford's illustration of Nightcrawler's hands and tail. OPPOSITE: Nightcrawler circus posters, concept, and design by Guy H. Dyas, line art by Adrien Van Viersen, color and graphics by Dianne Chadwick. Many original circus posters were created for the film and used as set decoration in the abandoned church to give a glimpse of Nightcrawler's past as a circus performer.

"There's a spring inside the tail harness that gives Nightcrawler's tail six different qualities of movement. It's based on the premise of gravity and movement, so rather than trying to puppet it with strings we let his own body motion manipulate the tail to create a very natural look. Each of the six different armature wires in the tail is machined at a different taper so that it can bend for wrapping around a tree or raise the tail straight up over his head."

—GORDON SMITH

"Nightcrawler's facial scars are based on conjuring symbols that have been around for thousands of years. Each symbol conjures a different kind of angel."
—GORDON SMITH

ABOVE: Church interior illustration by Collin Grant. LEFT: Alan Cumming in full makeup as the very religious Nightcrawler.

ABOVE LEFT: Night-crawler peers down from the church rafters. ABOVE RIGHT: Jean Grey and Storm enter the church. RIGHT: The X-Men's first encounter with Night-crawler. Photo by Director of Photography Tom Sigel. BELOW LEFT: The blue lights on the dangling Nightcrawler are used by special effects artists to help digitally attach his tail.

RIGHT: The Church's antechamber—decorated with Night-crawler's collection of circus posters—is where he hides and spends most of his time. Photos by Guy H. Dyas.

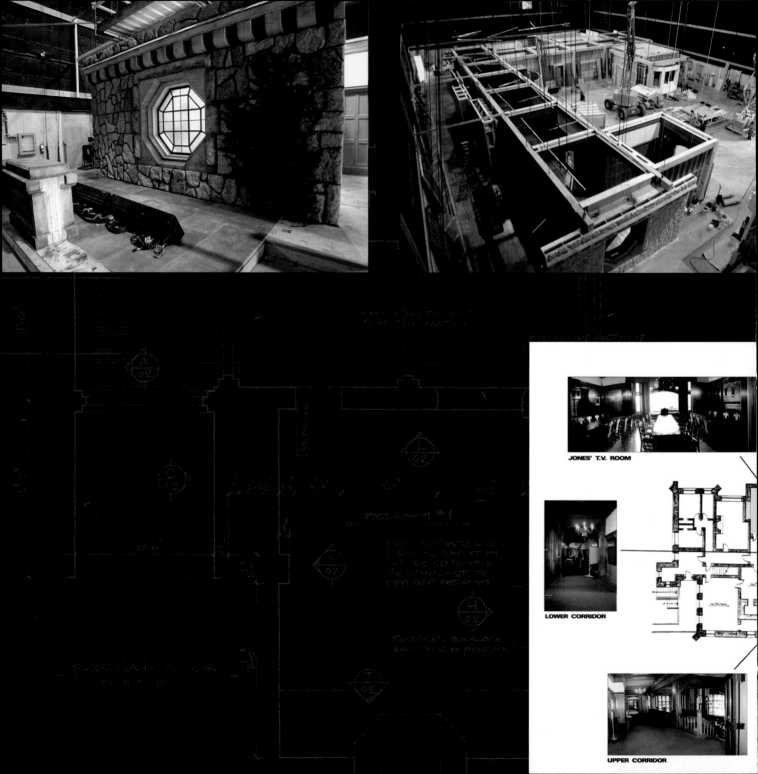

JONES' T.V. ROOM

LOWER CORRIDOR

UPPER CORRIDOR

X-MANSION

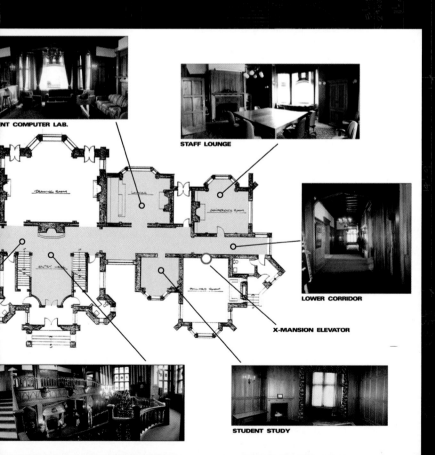

COMPUTER LAB.

STAFF LOUNGE

LOWER CORRIDOR

X-MANSION ELEVATOR

STUDENT STUDY

The Xavier Mansion set was recreated to resemble the first film's X-Mansion interior and to accommodate the elaborate attack scene and stunts of *X2*. The new set added a kitchen, bedrooms, and corridors with secret trapdoors as dictated by the script. The mansion's exterior shots were filmed at an historic mansion on Victoria Island called "Royal Roads." This location in Vancouver, B.C., was only reachable by plane and by boat.

TOP LEFT: Exterior wall and window of Xavier's Mansion. TOP CENTER: The mansion set under construction. TOP RIGHT: Wide angle view of X-Mansion's main corridors set. Photos by Guy H. Dyas. NEAR LEFT: Plan of Xavier's Mansion location and room layout, by Guy H. Dyas. BACKGROUND: Set plan of Xavier's Mansion by Alan Galajda.

ABOVE RIGHT: Royal Roads Mansion. Photo by Guy H. Dyas. ABOVE: Photoshop-manipulated illustration of the X-Mansion exterior by Mark Goerner. LEFT: Concept illustration interior of X-Mansion garage by Mark Goerner. BOTTOM: The finished X-Mansion garage set housing Xavier's collection of vintage sports cars and Cyclops' Mazda RX-8. Photo by Guy H. Dyas. RIGHT: Concept art for X-Mansion's secret helipad that appeared in an early draft of the script. Large illustration by Nathan Schroeder, inset by Mark Goerner.

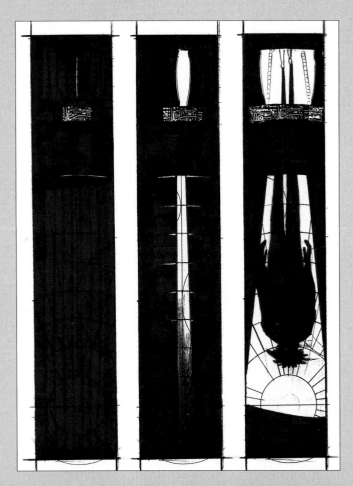

The Danger Room is a well-known room in the X-Mansion the film-makers considered for *X-Men* and *X2*. ABOVE: Storyboard sequence of Wolverine in the Danger Room by Adam Kubert. RIGHT and OPPOSITE: Concept illustrations of the Danger Room in use by Wolverine and the Danger Room's control room.

Artist: Adam Kubert

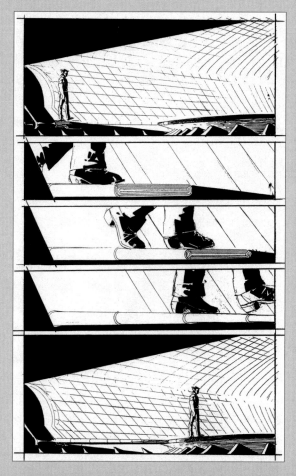

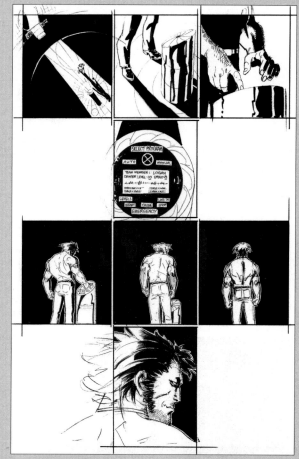

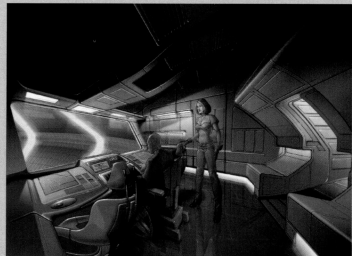

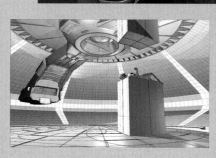

LEFT: 3D animatic frames for the Danger Room sequence considered for *X2*.

ABOVE: Concept illustration by Nathan Schroeder depicting an early version of Stryker's troops attacking the X-Mansion.

LEFT: The X-Mansion is breached. RIGHT: Costume illustration by Dean Sheriff of Stryker's troops' uniforms worn during the attack on the X-Mansion. BELOW: Logan prepares to defend the children. Photo by Dan Harris.

ABOVE: The underground corridors of the X-Mansion. RIGHT and BELOW RIGHT: Cerebro set under construction showing moveable walls positioned face to face, and as one larger section. The Cerebro set was built with movable wall pieces on either side of the entrance in order to accommodate any shooting angle. BELOW: Scale model of Cerebro set by Luke Freeborn. Photos by Guy H. Dyas. OPPOSITE: Two views of the completed Cerebro set.

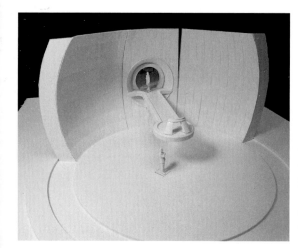

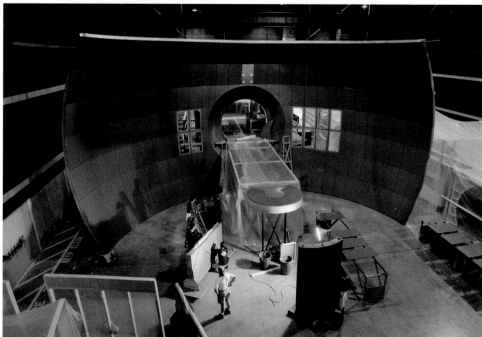

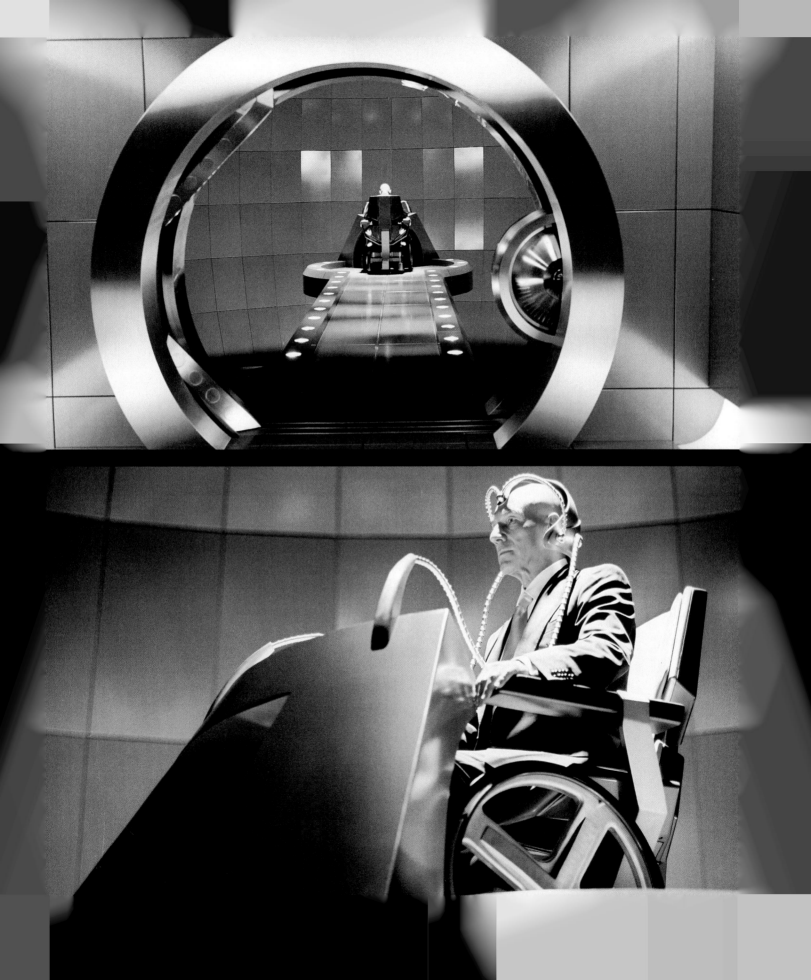

BG. SHIFTS

BOOM!

A - ANGLE PAST XAVIER ...THE GIRL FLASHES TO 143 AND BACK.. (O.S. "PROFESSOR!")

B - XAVIER LOOKS AROUND CONFUSED
— THE GIRL IS VERY AGITATED..

- ON THE OTHER SIDE OF THE CHASM ...A RUMBLE ... METAL PLATES & DEBRIS START RAINING DOWN...

- PAST STORM & NIGHTCRAWLER
- PUSH IN TO CLOSE UP...

⑨

C ...STORM TURNS TO NIGHTCRAWLER ...

WIDE ...HE PUTS HIS ARMS HER AND THEY BAMF...

BAMF!

BAMF!

- BACK W/XAVIER AND THE GIRL — STORM & N.C. BAMF BETWEEN THEM...

- THE GIRL STARES ANGRILY...

⑩

- XAVIER TURNS ..."STORM ... I WAS JUST TRYING TO FIND YOU."

- STORM: "PROFESSOR, YOU HAVE TO STOP CEREBRO NOW"

- XAVIER: "I'M JUST LOCATING THE OTHERS ...AND SHOWING OUR FRIEND THE MUTANTS OF THE WORLD."

- THE LITTLE GIRL SMILES

⑪

STORM: "THESE AREN'T THE MUTANTS OF THE WORLD..."

- CLOSE ON XAVIER CONFUSED ...

- STORM: "PROFESSOR: NONE OF THIS IS REAL ...YOU HAVE TO SEE BEYOND IT"

- LITTLE GIRL: "DON'T LISTEN TO HER SHE'S LYING!"

⑫

56.X2

Artist: Brent Boates

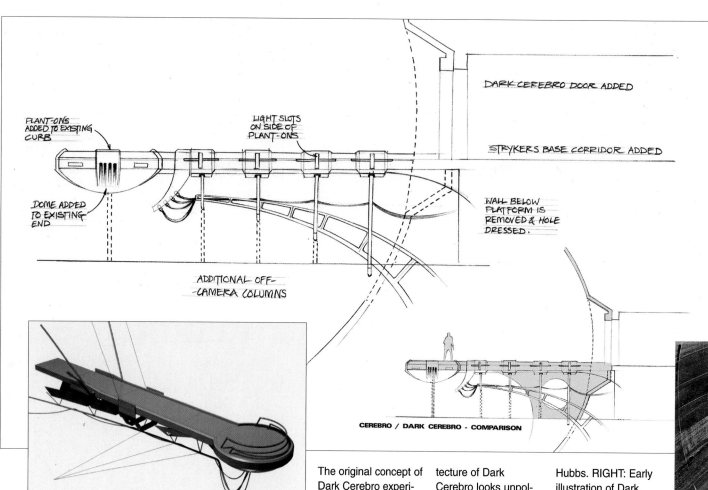

PLANT-ONS ADDED TO EXISTING CURB

LIGHT SLOTS ON SIDE OF PLANT-ONS

DARK CEREBRO DOOR ADDED

STRYKERS BASE CORRIDOR ADDED

DOME ADDED TO EXISTING END

WALL BELOW PLATFORM IS REMOVED & HOLE DRESSED.

ADDITIONAL OFF-CAMERA COLUMNS

CEREBRO / DARK CEREBRO - COMPARISON

The original concept of Dark Cerebro experimented with the idea of placing Xavier face to face with Mutant 143 on dual platforms, creating a mirror effect. Because Stryker's troops quickly built the replica of Cerebro inside of Stryker's base, the overall architecture of Dark Cerebro looks unpolished and somewhat dismantled. Without Magneto's help the result is far from being as flawless as Xavier's original Cerebro.

TOP RIGHT: Model of the dual-platform concept by Lawrence Hubbs. RIGHT: Early illustration of Dark Cerebro by Guy H. Dyas. TOP FAR RIGHT: Early concept illustration of Dark Cerebro by Nathan Schroeder showing Mutant 143 behind Xavier.

TOP: Elevation of Dark Cerebro set piece. ABOVE: Computer-generated models of Dark Cerebro platforms by Paul Ozzimo. RIGHT: Concept sketch of the final Dark Cerebro by Guy H. Dyas.

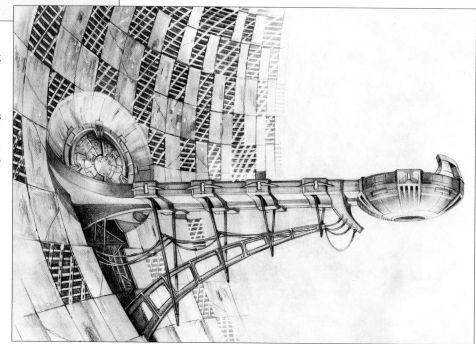

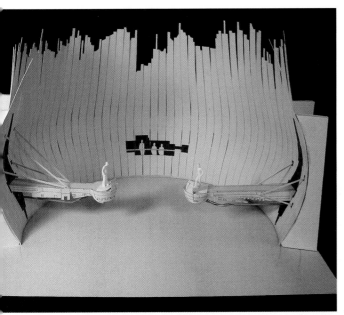

PATRICK STEWART

PROFESSOR X

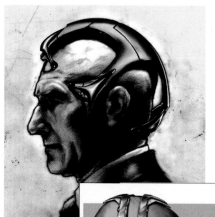

LEFT: An early concept illustration by Brentan Harron of Xavier's neural inhibitor device used in the film to restrain his mind-reading powers. The final design is seen below on a digital rendering of Patrick Stewart.

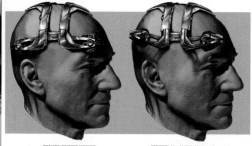

SIDE VIEW / INHIBITOR ACTIVATED

SIDE VIEW / sides of inhibitor hinge open for removal

FRONT VIEW

TOP/BACK VIEW

"The writers are very faithful to the origins of *X-Men*. But then they do something more that is also necessary to bring the story to film. They enhance and expand and develop and tweak those origins, giving them new dimension and new perspective."

—PATRICK STEWART

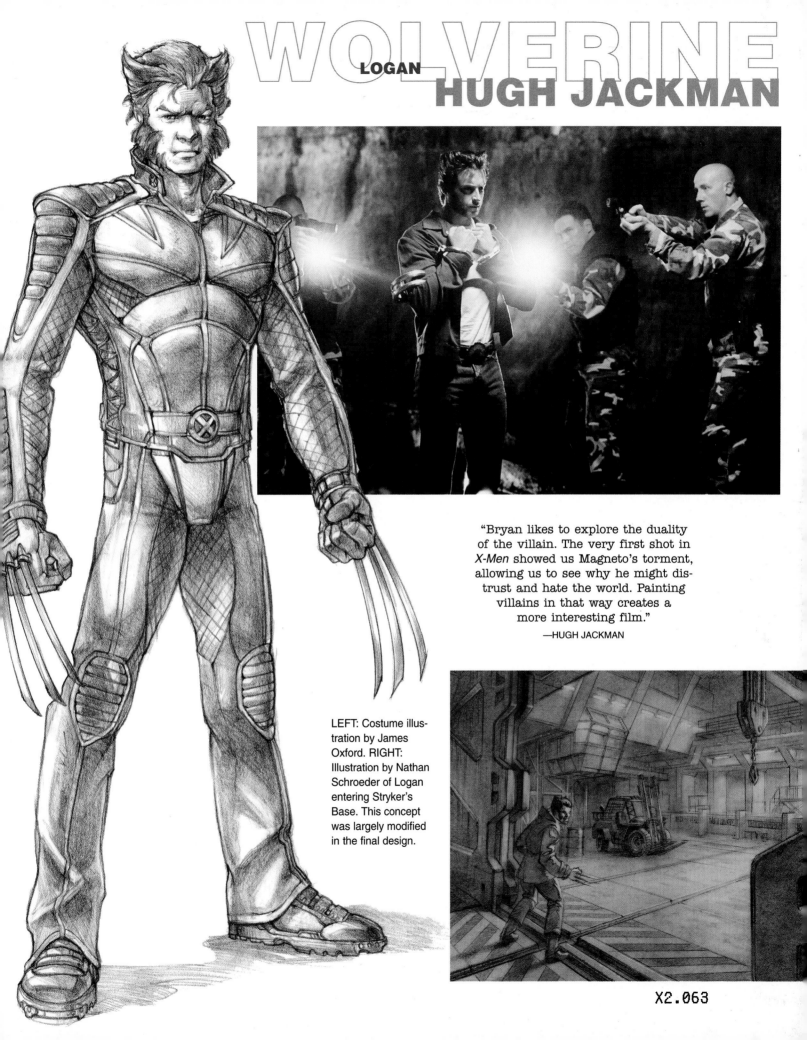

"Bryan likes to explore the duality of the villain. The very first shot in *X-Men* showed us Magneto's torment, allowing us to see why he might distrust and hate the world. Painting villains in that way creates a more interesting film."

—HUGH JACKMAN

LEFT: Costume illustration by James Oxford. RIGHT: Illustration by Nathan Schroeder of Logan entering Stryker's Base. This concept was largely modified in the final design.

Wolverine defends
the X-Mansion from
Stryker's invaders.

JEAN GREY
FAMKE JANSSEN

"Bryan made this into a movie that's a lot darker and edgier than your general comic book adaptation. He has a very unique way of working and knows exactly what he wants. It's very exciting, because it's always evolving—everything is being improved upon the entire time you're working."

—FAMKE JANSSEN

LEFT: Costume illustration for Jean Grey by James Oxford.

CYCLOPS
SCOTT SUMMERS
JAMES MARSDEN

Cyclops' visor in the first film was almost an exact copy of the one featured in the original comic book. By re-working its overall shape and color scheme and manufacturing the *X2* version out of lighter materials, James Marsden was afforded more freedom when it came to facial expression. A 3D scan of his head assured a perfect and comfortable fit.

RIGHT: Three concept illustrations of Cyclops' new visor by Brentan Harron. BELOW: Illustration by Brentan

Harron of Cyclops wearing the final visor design. LEFT: Computer-generated 3D models of Cyclops' new visor by Paul Ozzimo. BELOW LEFT: Actor James Marsden wearing the final visor design.

VERSION - 1

VERSION - 2

VERSION - 3

CAUTION:100ft DROP
PLEASE WAIT UNTIL TUNNEL IS FULLY EXTENDED
AND LOCKED BEFORE PROCEEDING

"In the first *X-Men* Rogue was really withdrawn because she'd just discovered her powers which were very new and quite scary. She was lost—a complete outsider. But by the end she'd been taken under the wing of the X-Men and Xavier. She'd found her home, which gave her a place to grow from."

—ANNA PAQUIN

RIGHT: Costume illustrations for Rogue by James Oxford.

STORM
HALLE BERRY
ORORO MUNROE

BELOW: Costume illustrations for Storm by James Oxford. The center and right images are early concepts for a shorter hairstyle for Storm.

PYRO

JOHN ALLERDYCE
AARON STANFORD

"A lot of people relate to the characters in *X-Men* because they're on the fringes of society. Kids growing up feel like that, and they relate to characters who are going through the same things they are. But instead of being helpless kids, the X-Men have knives coming out of their hands and can handle themselves."

—AARON STANFORD

LEFT: Pyro is holding a custom-designed lighter by Guy H. Dyas. The shark-tooth motif is an homage to one of Bryan Singer's favorite films, Steven Spielberg's *Jaws*. BELOW: Iceman, Wolverine, Pyro and Rogue at Bobby Drake's residence.

ICEMAN
BOBBY DRAKE
SHAWN ASHMORE

LEFT: The X-Kids in a confrontation at the Museum of Natural History. BELOW: Bobby Drake and Rogue in a scene with Logan and Ororo at the X-Mansion. RIGHT: Pyro's destructive ways captured by screen-writer Dan Harris.

MAGNETO
ERIK LEHNSHERR
IAN McKELLEN

LEFT and BELOW: Costume illustrations for Magneto by James Oxford. The new helmet design accentuates the Roman centurion influence of Magneto's original helmet while emphasizing the jawline and adding comfort to the overall fit.
RIGHT and BELOW RIGHT: Magneto in the Plastic Prison and James Oxford's costume drawing for Magneto's prison uniform.

"What's interesting about a character is not his extra special powers, but his inner life and inner strengths and the complications of his relationships with other people. I believe in Magneto. He's a man with a real past, a real dilemma and a real purpose for being alive. As for his abilities with regards to bending and attracting metal, in this sense, they are incidental to why I like him."
—IAN McKELLEN

MYSTIQUE
RAVEN DARKHOLME
REBECCA ROMIJN-STAMOS

"The make-up is a very, very difficult thing for Rebecca to go through. It started out as a ten-hour make-up, then we got it down to a six-and-a-half-hour make-up on the last film, and on this film we've gotten it down to four and a half hours. There are four girls working on her full time with no real break, and then when she's done she's being touched up all day long. It's a very stressful thing for her to have to go through. She's quite a spectacular-looking woman and the end result is very powerful on film."

—GORDON SMITH

PLASTIC PRISON

The original Plastic Prison set design had to be re-thought and expanded upon. There was a more varied use of plastic, some concrete elements were added, and the con- necting metal detection area was specifically designed to allow shooting from Magneto's perspective. One other challenge was to create an actu- al functioning access ramp that could expand and retract to connect the metal detection area to the plastic cell—something that was exclusively computer-generated in the original film. The use of the ramp is best seen during Magneto's escape.

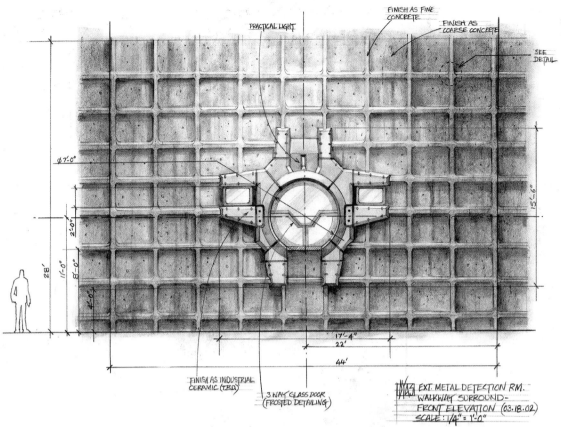

FINISH AS FINE CONCRETE
FINISH AS COARSE CONCRETE
PRACTICAL LIGHT
SEE DETAIL

Ø7'-0"
2'-0"
8'-0"
11'-0"
28'
4'-0"
15'-6"

17'-4"
22'
44'

FINISH AS INDUSTRIAL CERAMIC (T.B.D.)
3 WAY GLASS DOOR (FROSTED DETAILING)

DYAS EXT. METAL DETECTION RM.
WALKWAY SURROUND-
FRONT ELEVATION (03.18.02)
SCALE: 1/4" = 1'-0"

OPPOSITE TOP: Final touches to the Plastic Prison set on the eve of the first shoot. OPPOSITE MIDDLE: Interior of metal detection area. OPPOSITE BOTTOM: Shooting in progress in plastic cell showing Magneto waiting for Xavier's arrival. ABOVE: Detail of access tunnel joining the metal detection area to the plastic cell. Photos by Guy H. Dyas. ABOVE RIGHT: Elevation sketch of the exterior of the metal detection area and the access tunnel to the plastic prison, by Guy H. Dyas. RIGHT: View from the metal detection area window looking towards Magneto's plastic cell. Photo by Guy H. Dyas.

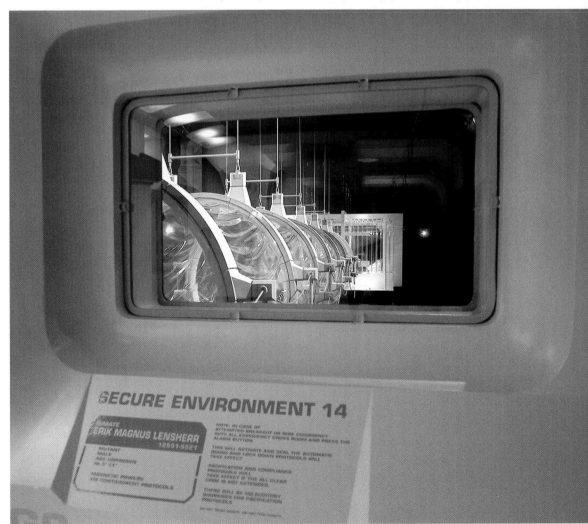

SECURE ENVIRONMENT 14

INMATE
ERIK MAGNUS LENSHERR   12551-5521

MUTANT
MALE
AGE UNKNOWN
IN 5'11"

MAGNETIC POWERS
SEE CONTAINMENT PROTOCOLS

NOTE: IN CASE OF ATTEMPTED BREAKOUT OR DIRE EMERGENCY WITH ALL EMERGENCY CROSS ROOM AND PRESS THE ALARM BUTTON

THIS WALL ACTIVATE AND SEAL THE AUTOMATIC DOORS AND LOCK DOWN PROTOCOLS WILL TAKE EFFECT

PACIFICATION AND COMPLIANCE PROTOCOLS WILL TAKE EFFECT IF THE ALL CLEAR CODE IS NOT EXTENDED

THERE WILL BE NO AUDITORY WARNINGS FOR PACIFICATION PROTOCOLS

X2.085

ABOVE: Magneto kills the guard Laurio and starts his escape using metal balls extracted from Laurio's blood. In order to get across the void left by the retracted access tunnel Magneto shapes the balls into a disc and thus travels to the other side. Conceptual illustration of this scene by Mark Goerner.

OPPOSITE TOP: Magneto in the metal detection area. Illustration by James Oxford. RIGHT: Exterior of the plastic cell looking back toward the metal detection area during the escape. Illustration by James Oxford. BELOW: Plastic prison before Magneto's escape. Illustration by Mark Goerner.

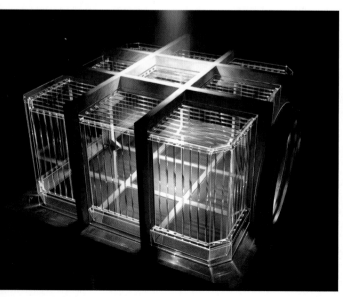

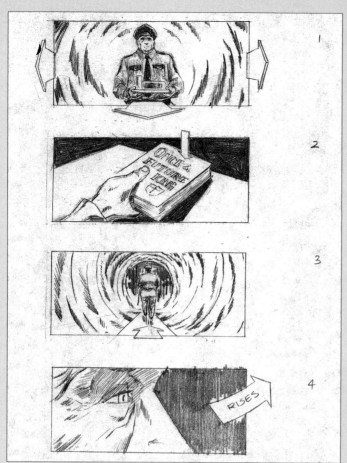

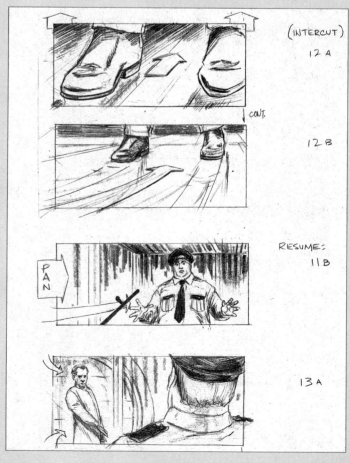

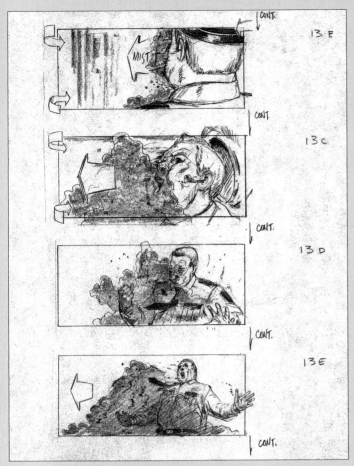

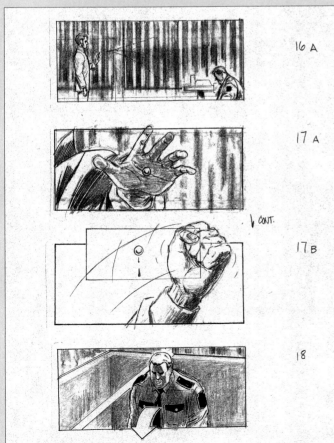

Artist: Rick Newsome

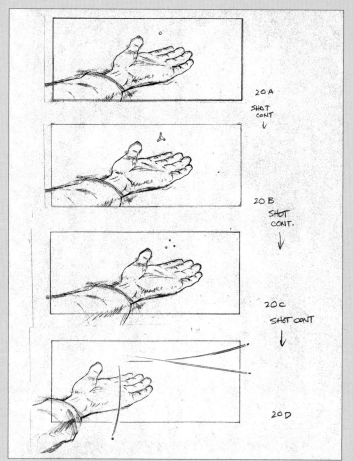

20A

SHOT
CONT

20B

SHOT
CONT.

20C

SHOT CONT

20D

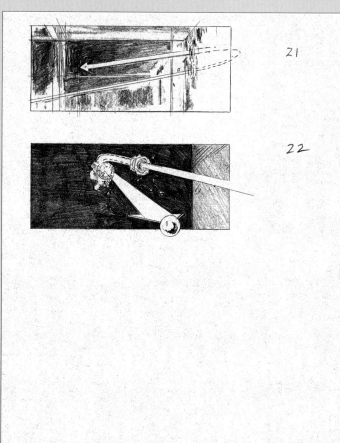

21

22

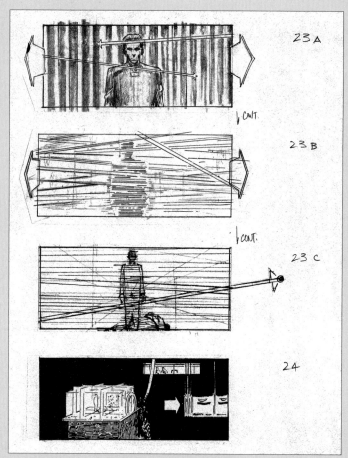

23A

CONT.

23B

CONT.

23C

24

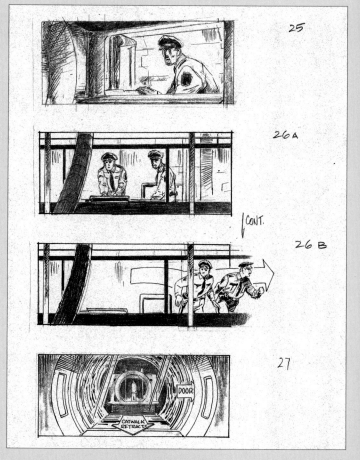

25

26A

CONT.

26B

27

DOOR

CATWALK
RETRACTS

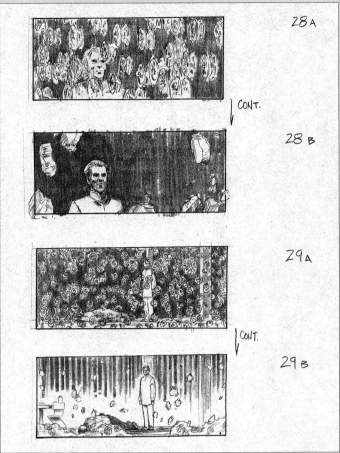

28A

CONT.

28B

29A

CONT.

29B

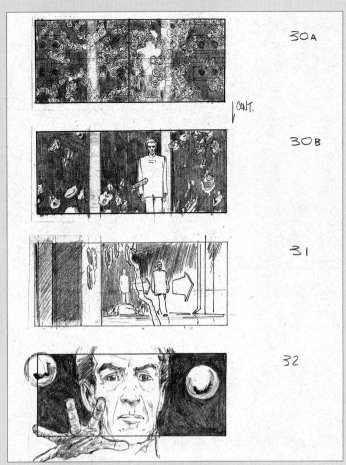

30A

CONT.

30B

31

32

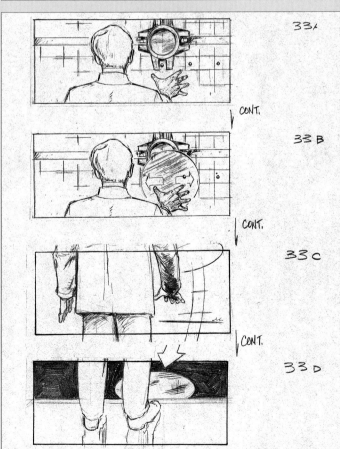

33A

CONT.

33B

CONT.

33C

CONT.

33D

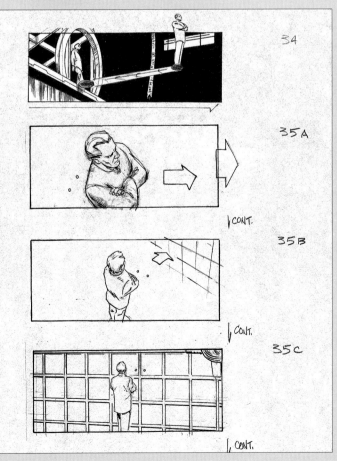

34

35A

CONT.

35B

CONT.

35C

CONT.

Artist: Rick Newsome

X2.091

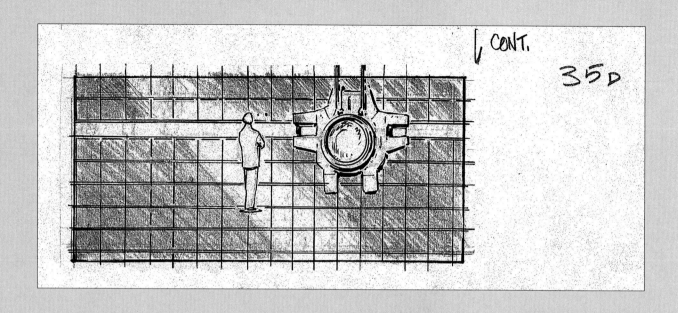

CONT.

35D

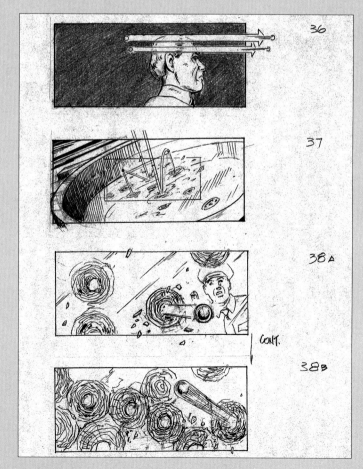

36

37

38A

CONT.

38B

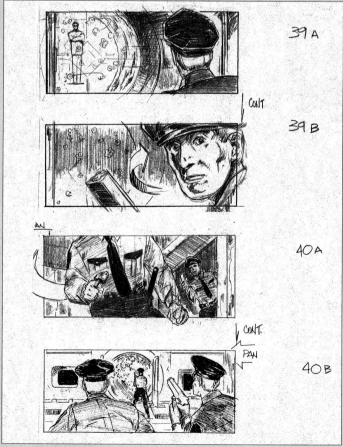

39A

CONT.

39B

40A

CONT.

PAN

40B

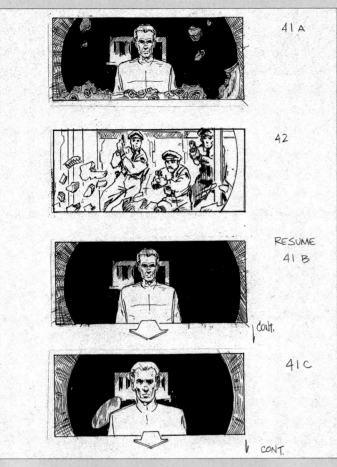

41 A

42

RESUME
41 B

CONT.

41 C

CONT.

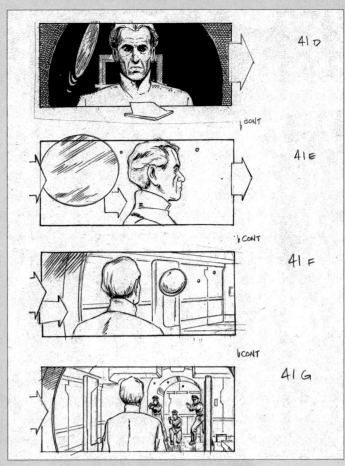

41 D

CONT

41 E

CONT

41 F

CONT

41 G

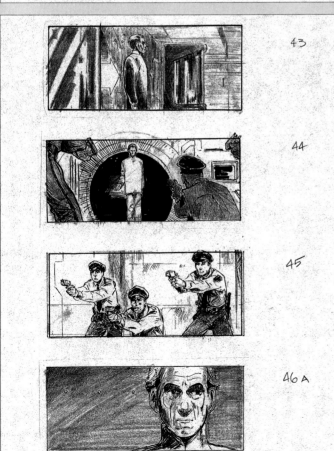

43

44

45

46 A

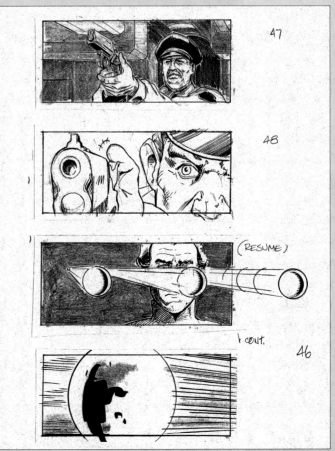

47

48

(RESUME)

CONT.

46

Artist: Rick Newsome

X2.093

Part 2
Augmentation

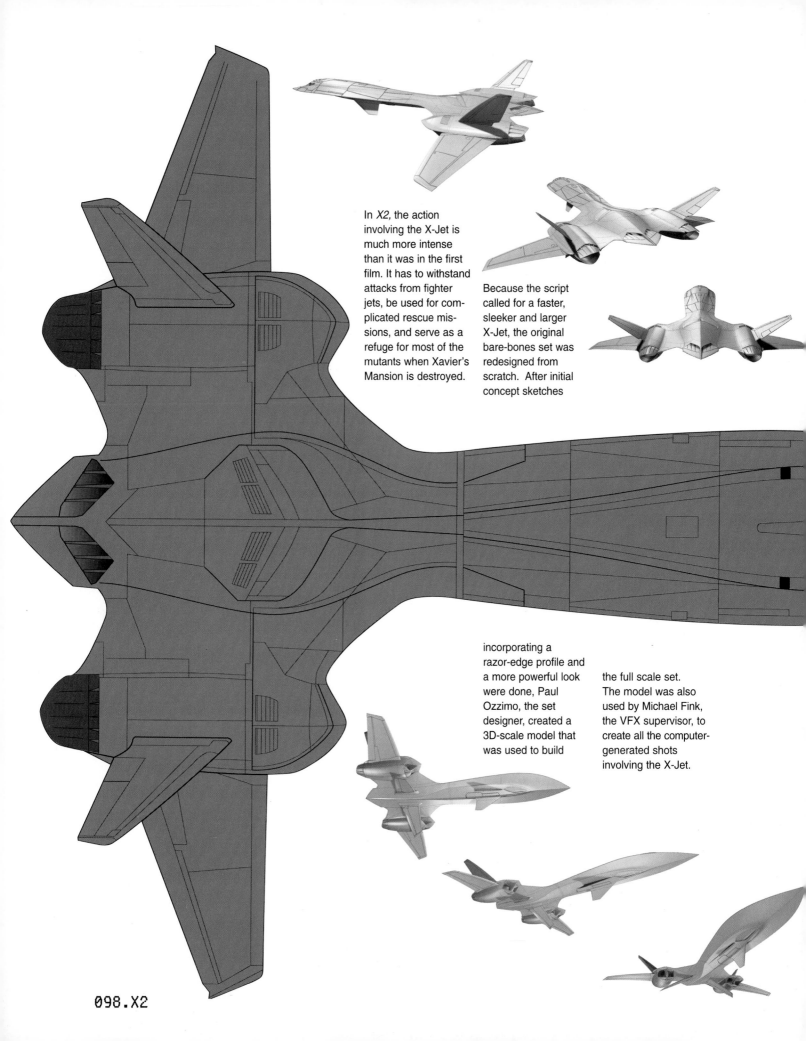

In *X2,* the action involving the X-Jet is much more intense than it was in the first film. It has to withstand attacks from fighter jets, be used for complicated rescue missions, and serve as a refuge for most of the mutants when Xavier's Mansion is destroyed.

Because the script called for a faster, sleeker and larger X-Jet, the original bare-bones set was redesigned from scratch. After initial concept sketches

incorporating a razor-edge profile and a more powerful look were done, Paul Ozzimo, the set designer, created a 3D-scale model that was used to build the full scale set. The model was also used by Michael Fink, the VFX supervisor, to create all the computer-generated shots involving the X-Jet.

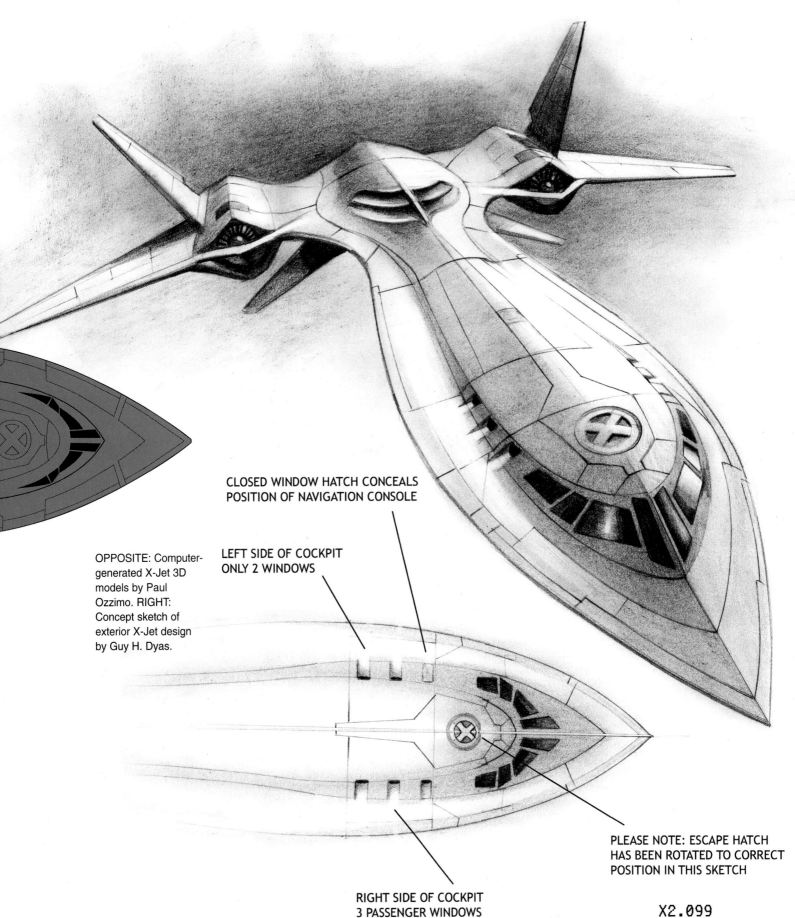

CLOSED WINDOW HATCH CONCEALS
POSITION OF NAVIGATION CONSOLE

LEFT SIDE OF COCKPIT
ONLY 2 WINDOWS

OPPOSITE: Computer-
generated X-Jet 3D
models by Paul
Ozzimo. RIGHT:
Concept sketch of
exterior X-Jet design
by Guy H. Dyas.

PLEASE NOTE: ESCAPE HATCH
HAS BEEN ROTATED TO CORRECT
POSITION IN THIS SKETCH

RIGHT SIDE OF COCKPIT
3 PASSENGER WINDOWS

X2.099

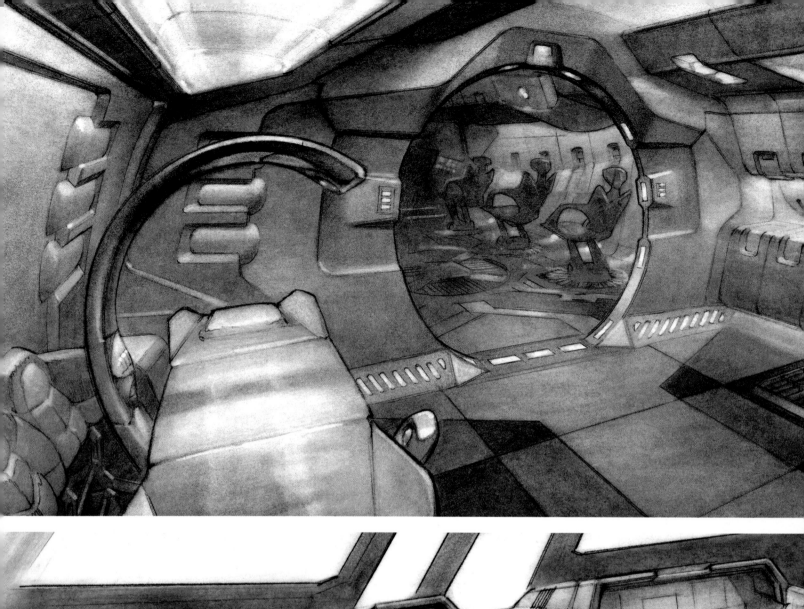

OPPOSITE ABOVE: Early concept showing the medical bay area which was later replaced with additional seating areas and the X-Men's combat suit storage units. Illustration by Nathan Schroeder. OPPOSITE BELOW: Detail of X-Jet's cockpit area. Illustration by Nathan Schroeder. ABOVE: Bryan Singer directs Ian McKellen and Aaron Stanford on the X-Jet set. RIGHT: Production designer Guy H. Dyas holding the resin scale model of the X-Jet. Photo by Bryan Singer. BELOW: Finished interior of the X-Jet set.

The interior of the X-Jet was designed to reflect the taste and personality of its captain, Storm, and to highlight her leadership and piloting skills. The X-Jet is extremely versatile and is designed with many compartments and modular sections. Its rear cargo can be equipped with aqua vehicles, and directly above the cockpit there's a circular hatch that gives access to the top of the X-Jet, which can also be used as an additional emergency exit.

OPPOSITE: Interior of the X-Jet cockpit. Illustration by Nathan Schroeder. OPPOSITE INSETS: Interior X-Jet set and Halle Berry as Storm at the X-Jet instrument panel.

ABOVE: 3D models of X-Jet interior by J. Andre Chaintrevil. These models are used by the Animatics department to create virtual spaces for the filmmakers to pre-visualize scenes.
LEFT: 3D model of X-Jet cockpit chair by J. Andre Chaintrevil. This model is used by the set de-partment to construct the chairs by CNC (computer controlled) milling and traditional molding techniques.

X2.103

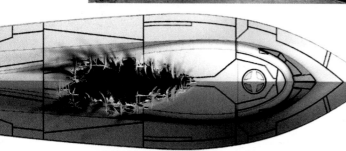

ABOVE: Early concept illustrating a missile entering from one side and going out the other, ripping a hole through the mid-section of the X-Jet. Illustration by Nathan Schroeder. LEFT: Concept sketch by Guy H. Dyas of damage to the X-Jet from a fighter jet missile attack. BOTTOM: The final concept used in the film shows the hole, just above the cargo area, where Rogue is sucked out. Illustration by Nathan Schroeder with additional Photoshop retouches by Guy H. Dyas.

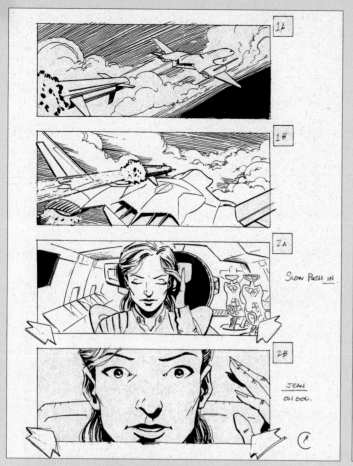

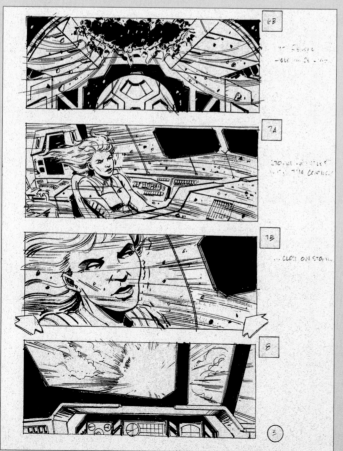

DOLLY PAST PYRO.

..TO NIGHTCRAWLER

TO BOBBY &
ROGUE.

..AS ROGUE
GETS SUCKED
TOWARD CEILING.

ROGUE
SLIPS

Artist: Adrien Van Viersen

X2.107

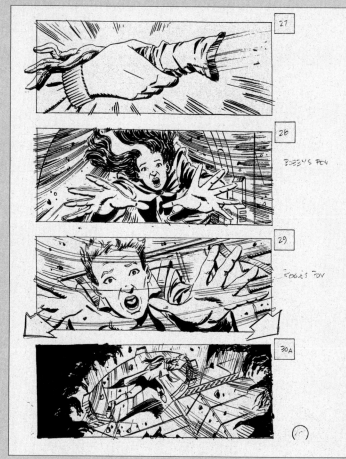

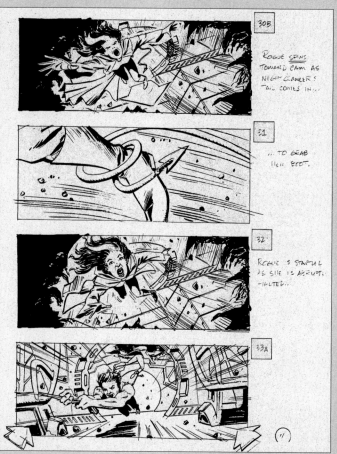

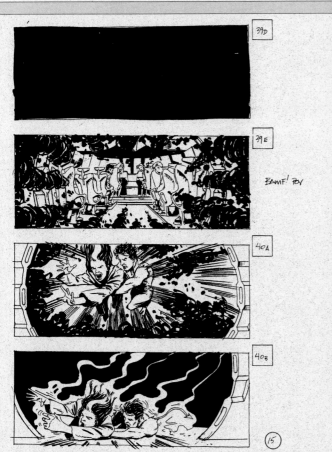

Artist: Adrien Van Viersen

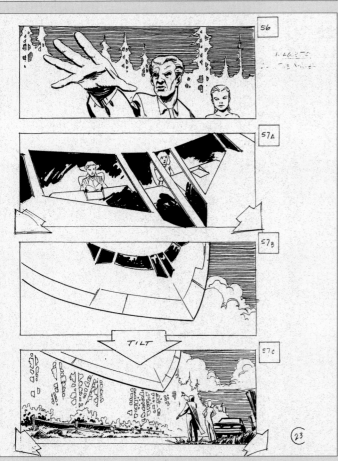

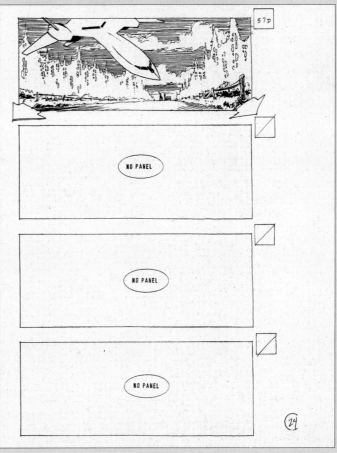

ABOVE: Illustration of X-Jet exit ramp by Nathan Schroeder. This early concept positioned the ramp on the side of the aircraft. Later a much more streamlined design put the exit on the underbelly of the X-Jet. LEFT: Famke Janssen and Hugh Jackman on the X-Jet exterior set built on location in the Canadian wilderness. BELOW: Overview sketch by Adrian Van Viersen of the X-Jet and camp site in a forest location. RIGHT: All of the camping equipment and tents are connected to the X-Jet via mechanical umbilical cords providing electrical power, telecommunications, and heat. Illustration by Nathan Schroeder. FOLLOWING PAGES: The Brotherhood and the X-Men join forces.

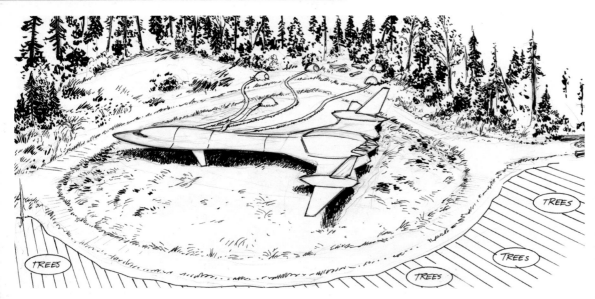

TREES

TREES

TREES

TREES

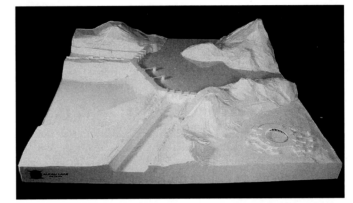

Wolverine's approach to the Old Alkali Lake facility brings up a lot of painful memories and stirs up his emotions. This is the pivotal moment when Wolverine discovers his origins. The stark concrete facades, bleak snow, and scale of the mountains are designed to accentuate his sense of loneliness.

LEFT INSET: Early concept sketch of the abandoned facility by Guy H. Dyas. LEFT: Concept sketch of Wolverine searching the dam's spillway for an entrance to Stryker's base, by Guy H. Dyas. ABOVE: Concept sketch of the escape route from Stryker's base, by Guy H. Dyas. RIGHT: Early concept model of the Alkali Lake and Dam by Luke Freeborn. BELOW RIGHT: Concept sketch of the Alkali Dam architecture by Guy H. Dyas.

These original, more elaborate, designs for Stryker's base were later abandoned by Bryan Singer because, above all else, he wanted to foster a sense of disappointment as Wolverine approaches the entranceway. Singer's idea was to have Wolverine see that there isn't much left of the building and that it won't bring him any of the answers he's been looking for. From a design standpoint, Stryker's base was redesigned not as a high-tech facility, but as an old building that Stryker renovated—a hidden facility where he could continue his cruel experiments on mutants. Illustrations by Guy H. Dyas.

ABOVE: Concept sketch by Guy H. Dyas of the abandoned base entrance. RIGHT: Finished set of the snow-covered entrance to the base. BELOW: The abandoned base entranceway under construction. Photos by Guy H. Dyas.

The architectural structures inside Stryker's base are purposely complex in order to create a lot of intersecting geometric shapes and to enhance the scale and perspective of the tunnels and ceilings. Concept sketches became 3D models for Bryan Singer to study for shooting angles. Then Photoshop illustrations were created as overlays onto the 3D models to determine not only form and scale for construction, but also to be able to discuss color, texture, and lighting with the DP, Newton Thomas Sigel.

OPPOSITE: Concept sketch by Guy H. Dyas of Wolverine walking down the spillway tunnel that leads to the entrance of Stryker's base. ABOVE: 3D model by Milena Zdravkovic of the spillway tunnel set, showing the doors opening. RIGHT: Photoshop illustration by Mark Goerner showing the interior of the loading bay in Stryker's base. BOTTOM: Photoshop illustration by Mark Goerner of loading bay door detail.

STRYKER'S BASE

OPPOSITE ABOVE: Photoshop illustration/3D model of Stryker's control room by Mark Goerner and Milena Zdravkovic. OPPOSITE BELOW: Finished set for Stryker's control room. Photo by Guy H. Dyas. LEFT: Kelly Hu as Yuriko with Stryker in the main corridors of Stryker's base. MIDDLE: Concept sketch by Guy H. Dyas of corridor leading to augmentation room. BELOW: Wolverine approaches the augmentation room. BACKGROUND: Set plan of augmentation room by Alan Galajd.

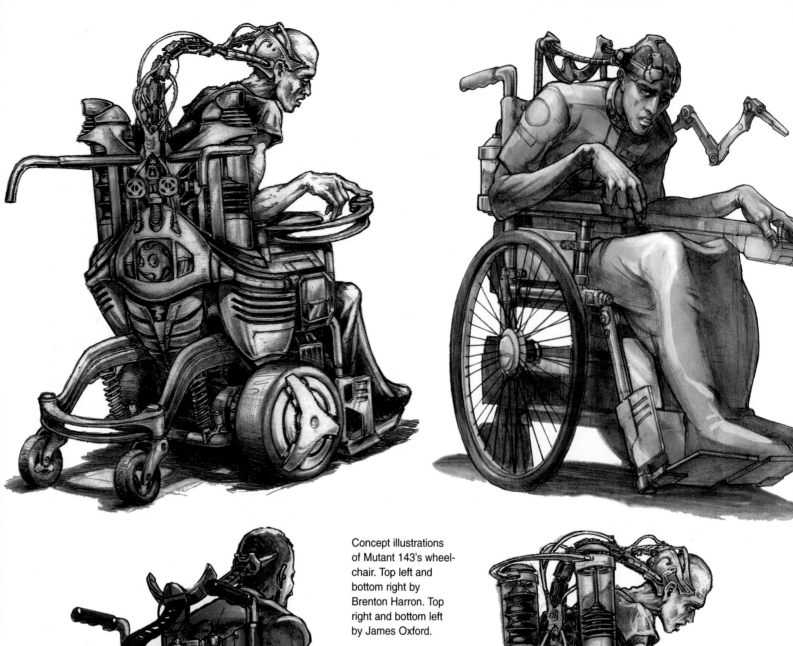

Concept illustrations of Mutant 143's wheelchair. Top left and bottom right by Brenton Harron. Top right and bottom left by James Oxford.

JASON

Mutant 143's wheel-chair construction was an elaborate process. Illustrations very quickly led to construction. By mixing hardware—everything from medical equipment to motorcycle parts—and spraying each part with a bronze and copper finish, the right look was finally achieved. Containing all sorts of moving parts, it resembles something out of a Jules Verne novel.

RIGHT: Michael Reid MacKay as Jason/Mutant 143. BELOW: Stryker leads Mutant 143 to Xavier inside Dark Cerebro.

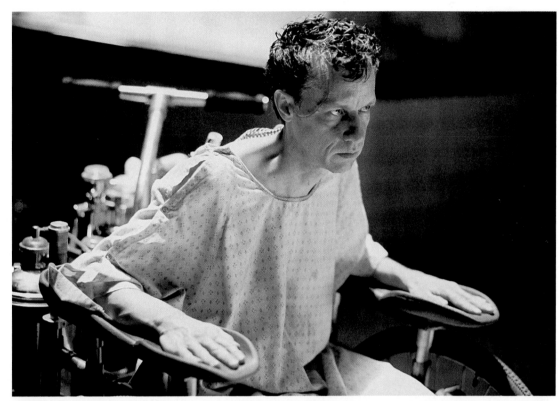

Throughout Stryker's Base there are several containment cells and holding spaces. Xavier's cell was designed to feel especially secure and claustrophobic, while Cyclops was restrained by using torturous chains and by altering his visor so that he can't use his laser beam.

OPPOSITE: Interior of Xavier's cell. ABOVE RIGHT: Cyclops' cell. Illustrations by Nathan Schroeder. CENTER: Detail of the children's containment cell. Photo by Guy H. Dyas. FAR RIGHT: Early concept sketch by Guy H. Dyas of one of the many mutant containment cells.

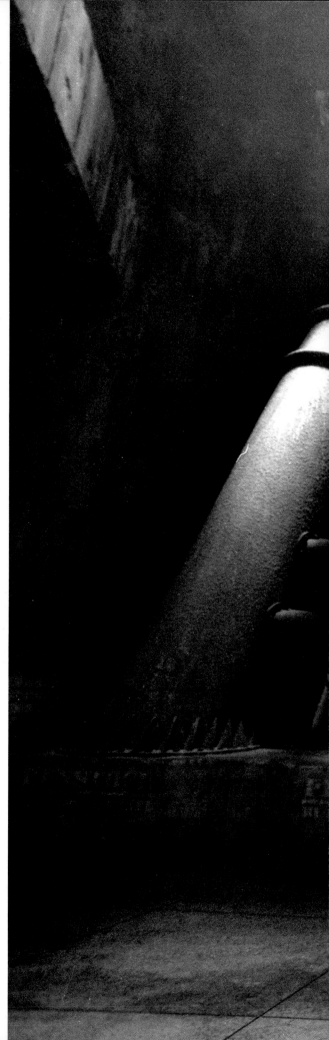

LEFT: View from the corridor and stairway looking down into the augmentation room at Stryker's Base. Photo by Guy H. Dyas. BELOW: Reverse view of the stairway entrance to the augmentation room in Stryker's Base. Photo by Guy H. Dyas.

ABOVE: Detail of operating tables in the augmentation room at Stryker's Base. Photo by Guy H. Dyas.
RIGHT: Guy H. Dyas in the augmentation room set on the first day of the augmentation room shoot.
BELOW: Concept sketches and wall elevations by Guy H. Dyas for the augmentation room at Stryker's Base.

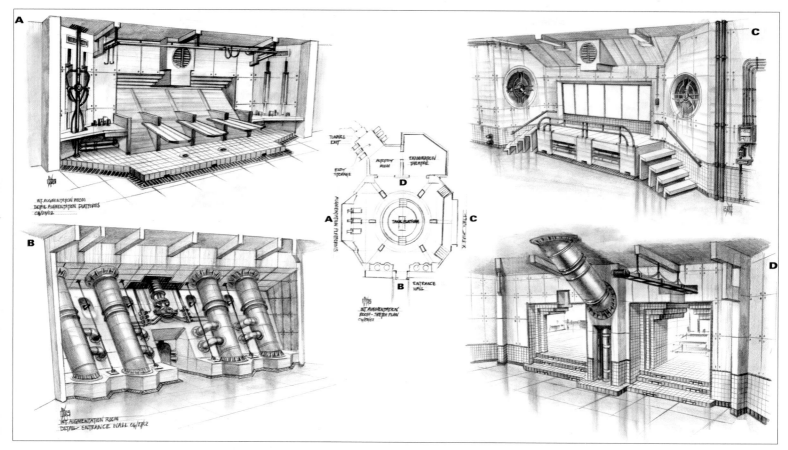

This set was a major undertaking to design and build. It involved precise planning for stunts and the end fight scene between Wolverine and Lady Deathstrike. The centrally located tank in which Wolverine was first experimented on is more visible than in the first film. And although it was redesigned—and built to Hugh Jackman's exact dimensions—the original circular window remains.

TOP: Wolverine in the augmentation room standing by the tank. ABOVE: Concept illustration of the augmentation room by Guy H. Dyas. RIGHT: X-ray wall on the augmentation room set. LEFT: Wide view of the tank area in the augmentation room. Photos by Guy H. Dyas.

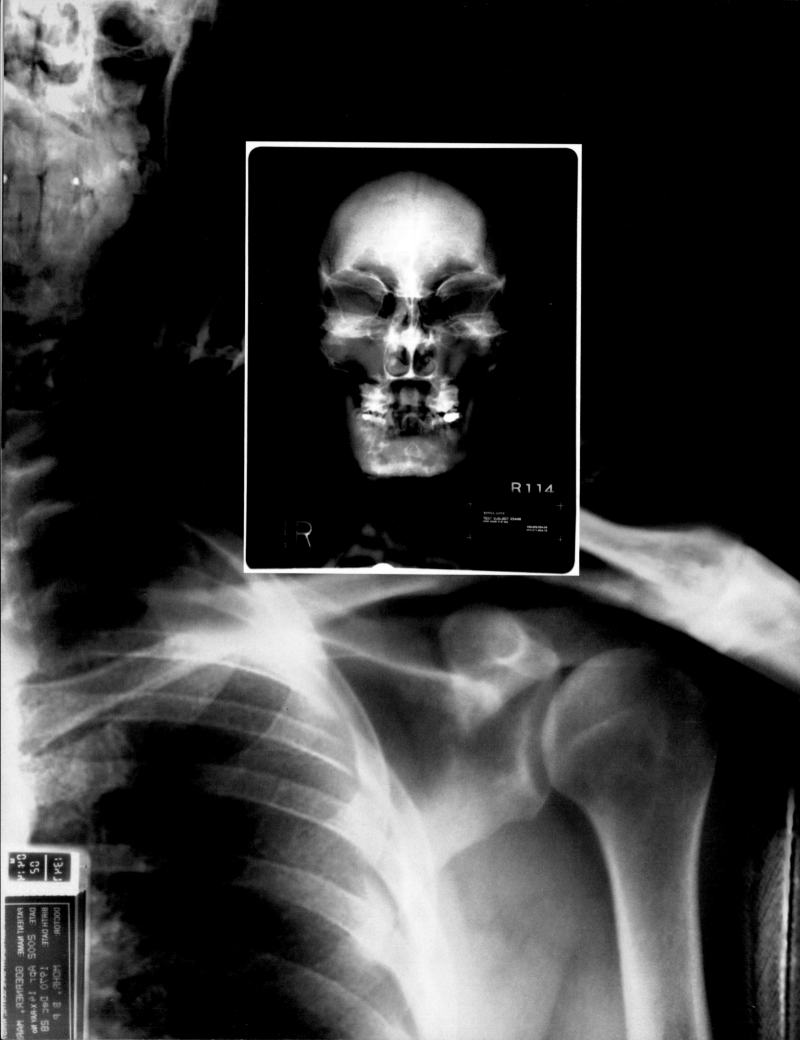

References to the
X-Men history were
included wherever
possible. For example
the X-ray wall pays
homage to famous
X-Men characters
such as Archangel
and Sabretooth.

LADY DEATHSRIK

YURIKO OYAMA
KELLY HU

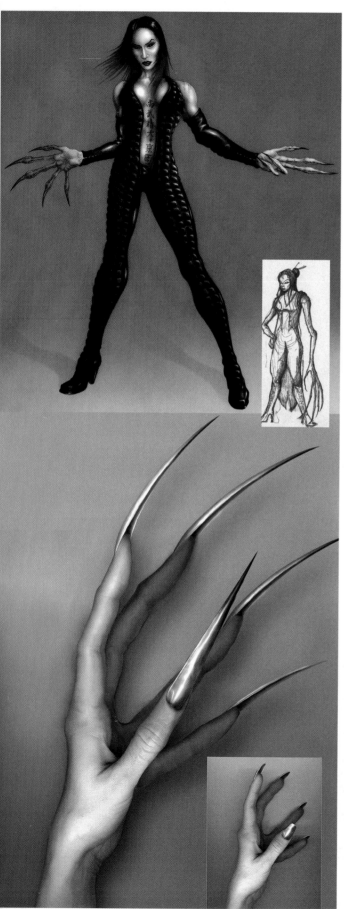

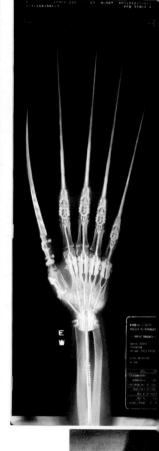

Early concepts of Lady Deathstrike's claws had the adamantium blades extending from her fingernails. In the film the blades are housed within her bone structure, much like Wolverine. Only her silver fingernails were kept from the original concept.

LEFT: Costume and character illustration of Lady Deathstrike and Photoshop illustration of Lady Deathstrike's adamantium claws by Jean-François Mignault. LEFT INSET: Screenwriter Mike Dougherty's pen sketch for Lady Deathstrike. RIGHT: X-ray Photoshop illustration of Lady Deathstrike's hand and forearm. BELOW: Kelly Hu as Lady Deathstrike. Photo by DP Newton Thomas Sigel. FOLLOWING PAGES: The aftermath. Illustration by Guy H. Dyas.

"I am a black belt in karate and in the film I get to do a lot of fighting—a style of fighting we just sort of invented. The stunt choreographers weren't as interested in it looking so martial-artsy as just vicious—and yet very sleek."

—KELLY HU

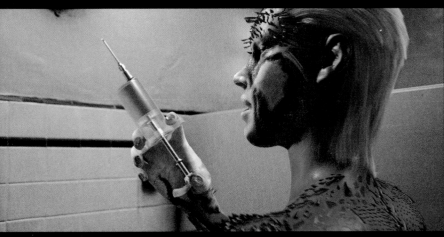

Mystique's more prominent role and more intimate transformations in *X2* prompted the special effects house, Kleiser-Walczak, to refine the 3D-morphing techniques they had developed for *X-Men*. An extremely detailed computer model of actress Rebecca Romijn-Stamos with anatomically correct musculature and skin deformations was created, and advanced rendering techniques—including high dynamic range environment maps, global illumination, and ambient occlusion passes—helped create the photoreal "synthespian" Mystique.

ABOVE: Kleiser-Walczak senior visual effects supervisor Frank E. Vitz (standing) confers with lighting supervisor Leonardo Quiles. Photo by Svetla Belcheva.

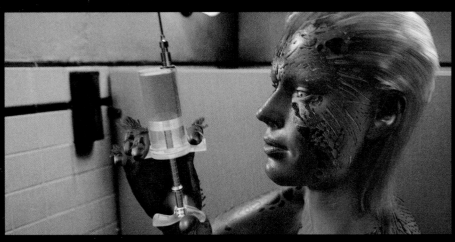

Numerous special effects technicians combined forces to bring the powers of the X-Men to the screen: Nightcrawler's Bamfing and gymnastics, Storm's weather fronts, Pyros control of fire, and the mutation of Collossus' flesh.

FAR LEFT: Concept art of Colossus' skin transformation by Jean-François Mignault.

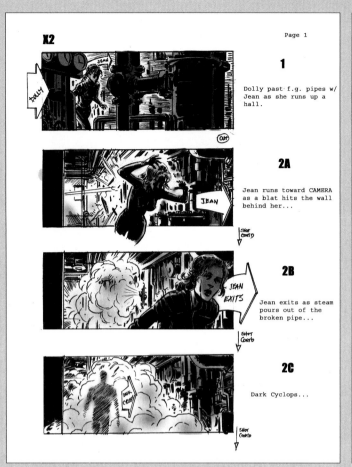

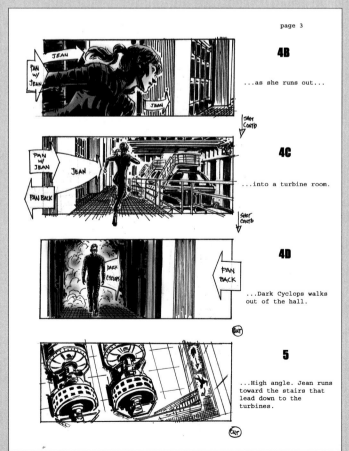

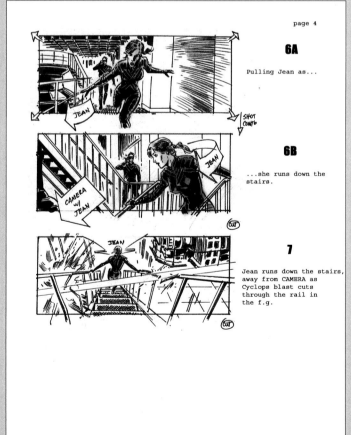

X2

Page 1

1

Dolly past f.g. pipes w/ Jean as she runs up a hall.

2A

Jean runs toward CAMERA as a blat hits the wall behind her...

2B

Jean exits as steam pours out of the broken pipe...

2C

Dark Cyclops...

page 2

2D

...emerges from the steam and fires.

3A

Jean enters frame then ducks...

3B

...avoiding the blast.

4A

Jean gets to her feet and runs toward CAMERA. Pan with her...

page 3

4B

...as she runs out...

4C

...into a turbine room.

4D

...Dark Cyclops walks out of the hall.

5

...High angle. Jean runs toward the stairs that lead down to the turbines.

page 4

6A

Pulling Jean as...

6B

...she runs down the stairs.

7

Jean runs down the stairs, away from CAMERA as Cyclops blast cuts through the rail in the f.g.

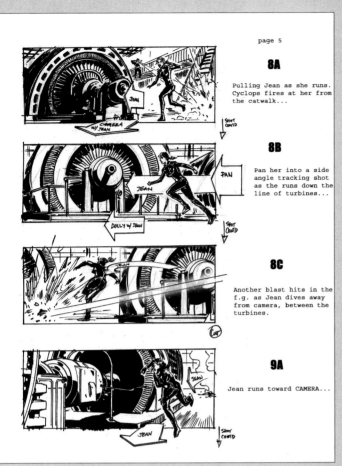

page 5

8A

Pulling Jean as she runs. Cyclops fires at her from the catwalk...

8B

Pan her into a side angle tracking shot as the runs down the line of turbines...

8C

Another blast hits in the f.g. as Jean dives away from camera, between the turbines.

9A

Jean runs toward CAMERA...

page 6

9B

...stopping in CU.

10

Angle over Jean. A dead end.

11A

Resume angle on Jean.

11B

She turns. Cyclops has a clear shot through the gap in the turbine.

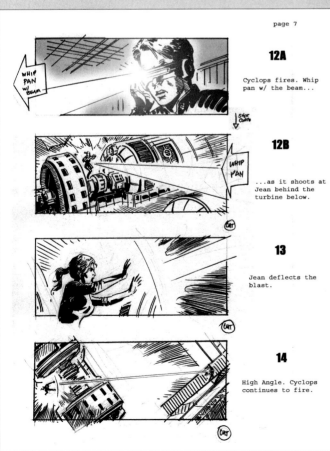

page 7

12A

Cyclops fires. Whip pan w/ the beam...

12B

...as it shoots at Jean behind the turbine below.

13

Jean deflects the blast.

14

High Angle. Cyclops continues to fire.

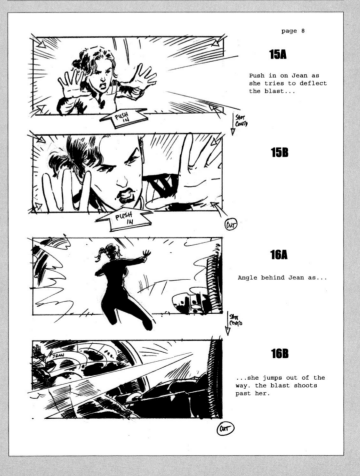

page 8

15A

Push in on Jean as she tries to deflect the blast...

15B

16A

Angle behind Jean as...

16B

...she jumps out of the way. the blast shoots past her.

Artist: Gabriel Hardman

LEFT: The full-size generator room set (a modified existing power station). Photo by Dan Harris. TOP: Lead miniature designer Jack Edjourian. ABOVE: Mini-generator set being built at 1:6 scale (notice the can of Coke, center stage). BELOW: Ray Moore, Jason Kaufman, and Corey Burton of Grant McCune Design install mini-generators.

Designed to break apart on cue, these mini-pipes (12"–16" in diameter), mini-nuts-and-bolts and mini-rivets were built to mimic the underground full-scale set (see page 140). The destruction—involving break-away lead panels, high-pressure water nozzles, compressed air and 12,000 gallons of water—was driven by pneumatics and hydraulics and coordinated by two computer systems. ABOVE LEFT: Special effects supervisor Michael Fink and Bryan Singer on the miniature dam set. ABOVE RIGHT: Cracks appear in the mini-dam. RIGHT: Filming the mini dam's destruction. BELOW: The fully dressed and lit miniature generator room set.

OPPOSITE TOP: Storm rescues the X-Kids from their cell. OPPOSITE BELOW: The X-Kids in their cell. RIGHT: Escape route from Stryker's base. Set piece built on location in Alberta, Canada. Photo by Guy H. Dyas. BELOW: Stryker chained to concrete wall by Magneto and left to die.

TWENTIETH CENTURY FOX Presents

In association with
MARVEL ENTERPRISES, INC.

X2

Directed by BRYAN SINGER

Screenplay by
MICHAEL DOUGHERTY & DAN HARRIS

Story by BRYAN SINGER & DAVID HAYTER
and ZAK PENN

Produced by
LAUREN SHULER DONNER
RALPH WINTER

Executive Producers
AVI ARAD
STAN LEE
TOM DeSANTO

Executive Producer BRYAN SINGER

Director of Photography
NEWTON THOMAS SIGEL, ASC

Production Designer GUY HENDRIX DYAS

Film Editor JOHN OTTMAN

Co-Producers
ROSS FANGER
KEVIN FEIGE

Visual Effects Supervisor MICHAEL FINK

Special Make-up Design GORDON SMITH

Music by JOHN OTTMAN

Costume Designer LOUISE MINGENBACH

PATRICK STEWART
HUGH JACKMAN
IAN McKELLEN
HALLE BERRY
FAMKE JANSSEN
JAMES MARSDEN
REBECCA ROMIJN-STAMOS
BRIAN COX
ALAN CUMMING
BRUCE DAVISON
SHAWN ASHMORE
AARON STANFORD
KELLY HU
and ANNA PAQUIN
KATIE STUART
KEA WONG

Casting by ROGER MUSSENDEN, CSA

THE DONNERS' COMPANY/BAD HAT HARRY
Production

A BRYAN SINGER Film

Unit Production Manager .... ROSS FANGER
Unit Production Manager .... STEWART BETHUNE
First Assistant Director .... LEE CLEARY
Second Assistant Director .... DAVID K. ARNOLD
Associate Producer .... DAVID GORDER

CAST

Professor Charles Xavier .... PATRICK STEWART
Logan/Wolverine .... HUGH JACKMAN
Eric Lehnsherr/Magneto .... IAN McKELLEN
Storm .... HALLE BERRY
Jean Grey .... FAMKE JANSSEN
Scott Summers/Cyclops .... JAMES MARSDEN
Mystique .... REBECCA ROMIJN-STAMOS
William Stryker .... BRIAN COX
Kurt Wagner/Nightcrawler .... ALAN CUMMING
Senator Kelly .... BRUCE DAVISON
Rogue .... ANNA PAQUIN
John Allerdyce/Pyro .... AARON STANFORD
Bobby Drake/Iceman .... SHAWN ASHMORE
Yuriko Oyama/Deathstrike .... KELLY HU
Kitty Pryde .... KATIE STUART
Jubilee .... KEA WONG
Jason 143 .... MICHAEL REID MACKAY
Little Girl 143 .... KEELY PURVIS
Colossus .... DANIEL CUDMORE
Jones .... CONNOR WIDDOES
Artie .... BRYCE HODGSON
Siryn .... SHAUNA KAIN
President McKenna .... COTTER SMITH
Steven Drake .... ALFRED E. HUMPHREYS
Madeline Drake .... JILL TEED
Ronny Drake .... JAMES KIRK
Mitchell Laurio .... TY OLSSON
Museum Teenager #1 .... GLEN CURTIS
Museum Teenager #2 .... GREG RIKAART
Cop #1 (Lead Cop) .... MARK LUKYN
Cop #2 .... KENDALL CROSS
Plastic Prison Guard .... MICHASHA ARMSTRONG
Federal Bldg. Cleaning Twin #1 .. ALFONSO QUIJADA
Federal Bldg. Cleaning Twin #2 .... RENE QUIJADA
Stryker Soldier Lyman .... PETER WINGFIELD
Stryker Soldier Smith .... STEPHEN SPENDER
Stryker Soldier #1 .... AARON DOUGLAS
Stryker Soldier #2 .... COLIN LAWRENCE
Stryker Soldier Wilkins .... DYLAN KUSSMAN
T.V. Host .... DAVID KAYE
Dr. Shaw .... CHARLES SIEGEL
Dr. Hank McCoy .... STEVE BACIC
White House Agent (Lead Agent) MICHAEL DAVID SIMMS
Oval Office Agent Cartwright .... ROGER R. CROSS
Oval Office Agent Fabrizio .... DAVID FABRIZIO
White House Checkpoint Agent .... MICHAEL SOLTIS
Whitehouse Tour Guide .... CHIARA ZANNI
News Reporters .... TED FRIEND, MI-JUNG LEE,
MARRETT GREEN, JILL KROP
X-Kids (Captured) .... NOLAN FUNK,
DEVIN DOUGLAS DREWITZ,
JERMAINE LOPEZ, SIDEAH ALLADICE
Stryker Soldier .... JASON S. WHITMER
Stryker Soldier .... AARON PEARL
Stryker At Age 40 .... BRAD LOREE
Augmentation Room Doctor .... SHERI G. FELDMAN
Special Ops Agent .... RICHARD BRADSHAW
F-16 Fighter Pilot .... LORI STEWART
Chief Of Staff Abrahms .... KURT MAX RUNTE
Loading Bay Stryker Soldier #1 RICHARD C. BURTON
Loading Bay Stryker Soldier #2 . MICHAEL JOYCELYN
Cameraman .... BENJAMIN GLENDAY
President's Secretary .... JACKIE A. GREENBANK
Cop .... ROBERT HAYLEY
Stunt Coordinators ...... GARY JENSEN, JACOB RUPP,
MELISSA STUBBS, ERNEST JACKSON
Stunts .... KEVIN ABERCROMBIE,
DAVID ALEXANDER, CHARLES ANDRE,
IEISHA AUYEUNG, JAMES BAMFORD,
KEVIN BEENHAM, CHAD BELLAMY,
RICHARD L. BLACKWELL, ROB BOYCE,
JAKE BRAKE, JOHN BRANAGAN,
DUSTIN BROOKS, DENNIS BULL, JASON CALDER,
SYLVAIN CAMERON, YVES CAMERON,
KIRK CAOUETTE, BRETT CHAN, RAYMOND CHAN,
DOUG CHAPMAN, KELSI CHARTRAND,
LAURO CHARTRAND, DEAN CHO,
CHAD COSGRAVE, VINCE CRESTEJO,

JESSE JAMES DAVIDSON, MICHAEL DOSABRAIS,
DUANE DICKINSON, KYLE DOERKSEN,
MIKE DOPUD, JOE DESERRO, JIM DUNN,
WILLIAM EDWARDS, MARNY ENG, GLENN ENNIS,
MARY FALLICK, DANE FARWELL,
DUSTY FINKBEINER, JIM FINKBEINER,
CORBIN H. FOX, BEAU GIBSON, CORRY GLASS,
CHRISTOPHER GORDON, LARS DAVID OLLIE GRANT,
ALEX GREEN, JASE-ANTHONY GRIFFITH,
ROBERT HAYLEY, CRAIG HOSKING,
DAVE HOSPES, GASTON HOWARD, KIM HOWEY,
ALANA HUSBAND, CAROL JACKSON,
CHELSEA JACKSON, COULTON JACKSON,
DAVID JACOX, JAY JAUNCEY, BEN P. JENSEN,
ETHAN JENSEN, TREVOR JONES, BRAD KELLY,
KEN KIRZINGER, JON KRALT, MICHAEL LANGLOIS,
PAUL LAZENBY, RANDY LEE, DON LEW,
JAKE LOMBARD, BRAD LOREE,
DEB MACATUMPAG, J.J. MAKARO, KIT MALLET,
JASON MARTIN, BRAD MATHESON,
DAN McLAREN, KIRK McMEEKAN,
MIKE MITCHELL, PHILLIP MITCHELL,
GIORGIO MIYASHITA, WILLIAM MORTS,
JOVAN NENADIC, SCOTT NICHOLSON,
VICKI PHILLIPS, SHAWN ORR,
EFOSA OTUOMAGIE, GERALD PAETZ,
RICK PEARCE, TERRANCE L. PEREGOODOFF,
FRED PERRON, DARRYL QUON, JASON RAND,
DAN REDFORD, JEFFREY C. ROBINSON,
MIKE ROSELLI, JUSTIN SAIN, RAYMOND SAMMEL,
CHRISTOPHER SAYOUR, TRICH SCHILL,
JEFF SCRUTTON, MARK SETER, GREG SMRZ,
MELODY SODERQUIST, HEATH STEVENSON,
BILL STEWART, SHAWN STEWART,
VICKI THIGMAN, FRANK TORRES,
ROSS UISDEAN, ANGELA UYEDA,
RENE VAN HULLEBUSH, LORI VELISEK,
ATTILA VEZINA, TUCKER VEZINA, CLAY VIRTUE,
MARSHALL VIRTUE, PAUL WU, MATT YANAGIYA
Co-Film Editor .... ELLIOT GRAHAM
Production Supervisor .... JASON McGATLIN
Supervising Art Director .... GEOFF HUBBARD
Art Director .... HELEN JARVIS
Assistant Art Directors .... BARBARA WILSON
BRENTAN HARRON
Set Decorator .... ELIZABETH WILCOX
Assistant Set Decorators .... IGNACIO McBURNEY
RON SOWDEN
Lead Set Dressers .... MATT REDDY
GORDON BRUNNER
Lead Set Designer .... LAWRENCE HUBBS
Set Designers .... NANCY BROWN,
J. ANDRE CHAINTREVIL, LUKE FREEBORN,
ALLAN GALAJDA, DAN HERMANSEN,
ANDREW LI, MARGOT READY, DEAN WOLCOTT,
MILENA ZDRAVKOVIC
Art Department Coordinators ...... FRANZISKA KELLER
AIMEE ROUSEY
Model Maker .... CRICKET PRICE
Sculptor .... JAMES H. JONES
Illustrators .... JAMES OXFORD, MARK GOERNER,
JEAN-FRANCOIS MIGNAULT, PAUL OZZIMO,
NATHAN SCHROEDER, DEAN SHERRIFF
Graphic Designers ...... RAY LAI, DIANNE CHADWICK,
ERIC ROSENBERG
Storyboard Artists .... ROBERT CONSING,
BRENT BOATES, TREVOR GORING,
COLLIN GRANT, GABRIEL HARDMAN,
DAVID MACLEAN, RICHARD NEWSOME,
ADRIEN C. VAN VIERSEN

Second Second Assistant Director .. GERROD SHULLY
Third Assistant Director .... SILVER BUTLER
Trainee Assistant Directors .... GARY HAWES
ASHLEY BELL
On Set Dresser .... PATRICK KEARNS
Set Dressers .... CHAD CHILIBECK, ANN ROWLEY,
ROSS WAHL, J.P. BAGSHAW, DENNIS SIMARD,
BRENT BENNETT, MICHAEL BETHUNE

Set Decoration Coordinator......................URA JONES
Steadicam Operator/B Camera ....TIM MERKEL
First Assistant Camera – A Camera ....JIMMY JENSEN
First Assistant Camera –B Camera.....SEAN HARDING
Second Assistants Camera ....DAVID LOURIE
    DEAN MORIN
Loader ....MICHELLE HNILICA
Camera Trainees..........................CASEY HARRISON,
    HEIDI BUECKING, ADELLA ZELLER,
    MICHAEL GREEN
Still Photographers ....KERRY HAYES
    DOANE GREGORY
Sound Mixer ....ROB YOUNG, C.A.S.
Boom Person ....JON LAVENDER
Cable Person ....ANDY BISHOP
Video Assist ....JEFFREY CASSIDY
Assistant Video Replay..................DAVID KURVERS
Property Master.....................................JIMMY CHOW
Assistant Property Masters....CATHERINE LEIGHTON
    JASON LANDELS
Props Buyers.............................ANDREAS NIEMAN
    TRINITA WALLER
Assistant Props ....CLAUDIO PALAVECINO
Armourer...ROB FOURNIER
Script Supervisor ....CHRISTINE WILSON
Chief Lighting TechnicianTONY "NAKO" NAKONECHNYJ
Gaffer..DAVID TICKELL
Best Boys Electric ....JEFF HARVEY
    AVRON SHER
Lighting Board Operator..................KELLY MALONEY
Electricians......................................KEN W. ANDERSON,
    ANDREW PERESZLENYI, ROBIN HALL,
    DON KAZAKOFF
Generator Operator...........................JAY ANDERSON
Rigging Gaffer....................................JARROD TIFFIN
Best Girl – Rigging ....CHANTAL MORIN
Best Boy – Rigging............................JOHN PIROZOK
Key Grip..STEVE SMITH
Best Boy Grip ....GARY J. WILLIAMS
On Set Best Boy Grip..........................PAT WALLER
Dolly Grip – A Camera...............BRIAN JOHN BOUMA
Dolly Grip – B Camera.........................REID COHOON
Company Grips........TIM MILLIGAN, RICK STADDER,
    JAMES J. WILLIAMS, JAY RUPERT,
    GERHARD YOUNG
Key Rigging Grip ....ROBIN JOBIN
Assistant Key Rigging Grip....BIPPIN KUMAR SAMMY
Rigging Grips..........................BUBBER GUENTHER,
    BOB WOLINSKI, DON QUINN, JULIEN BOSSE
X-Men Uniforms by ....JOSE FERNANDEZ
Assistant Costume Designer ....CATHY CRANDALL
Key Costume Coordinator ....GRACE ANDERSON
Costume Coordinator ....JANICE K. SWAYZE
Set Costume Supervisor ....ELIZABETH NEEDHAM
Costumers ....DEBBIE JUBA WINSTON,
    LAVONE NAPIER, MICHELE LYLE, CATHY DARBY,
    VIVIAN BAUMANN, DEBBIE HUMPHREYS,
    MARNIE ANDER, COURTNEY ANDERSEN
Key Costume Cutter ....NORMA HIEBERT DUFFY
Key Breakdown Artist....................DENISE GINGRICH
Stitcher/Builder..................................ROSALIE LEE
Key Costumer – L.A.................KRISTIN M. DANGL
Costume Supervisor – L.A....................PAUL LOPEZ
Cutter/Fitter.......................................KAREN NASER
Costumers ....TRISH SACCHI, CARIN RICHARDSON,
    MARIA SUNDEEN, STACIA LONG
Stitchers ....HAYDEE RAMIREZ, VAN HUA,
    AGAPI PAPAS, ANGELINA PADRON
Specialty Fabricator ....JILL TOMOMATSU
Make-Up Designer...................NORMA HILL-PATTON
Head Make-Up Artist...........................RITA CICCOZZI
Make-Up Artist ....ANGELA WOOD
Department Head – Hair......JENNIFER O'HALLORAN
Key Hair Stylist........................PAULINE L. TREMBLAY
First Assistant Hair Stylist ....NANCY STEYNS
Make-Up Artist for Halle Berry ....MARY BURTON

Special Make-Up Effects by:
FX SMITH INC. & COMPANY

Key Sculptor ....EVAN PENNY
Sculptor ....JOE VENTURA
Key Prosthetics ....JAY McCLENNEN,
    CAROLINE DEMOOY, ANN McLAREN
Prosthetics .....MARIANNE LOVINK, DAVID FOWLER,
    JULIE BOULE, MAYA KULENOVIC
Key Hair and Wigs Builder ....DONNA GLIDDON
Key Mechanical ....JAMES GAWLEY
Contact Lenses Provided by
    PROFESSIONAL VISION CARE, INC.
Tattoo Design..........................URBAN PRIMATIVE
Dental Prosthetics ....RA & ASSOCIATES, INC.
Studio Manager ....GIONILDA STOLEE
Vancouver Crew
Key Make-up ....JAYNE DANCOSE
    CHARLES C. PORLIER
Key Painter................................GILLIAN RICHARDS
Make-up ....MONICA HUPPERT
Contact Lens Technician.......BEVERLY A. MONCRIEF
2ND Unit Make-up Artists ....TOBY LINDAIA,
    CHRISTOPHER PINHEY, LEANNE PODAVIN,
    MARGARET YAWORSKI
Location Manager ....RINO PACE
Assistant Location Managers ....JAY ST. LOUIS
    JASON M. COLLIER, MARK VOYCE
Locations Trainee ....HANS DAYAL
Location Production Assistants ..SANDY McKECHNIE,
    TODD IRELAND, DAN KUZMENKO,
    KATARINA SAGANOVA, CLINT BUTLER,
    DAVID BURNEY, SEAN FINNAN, STEPHEN CHAN,
    LYNDSAY ANDERSON
Production Coordinator ....SHEENAH MAIN
Assistant Production Coordinators.....PAULA SIMSON,
    JENA NIQUIDET, NICOLE FLORIAN
Production Secretaries.......................JUDITH SWAN,
    AMY MORRISON, JANET GLOWA
Special Effects Coordinator ....MIKE VEZINA
Special Effects – Shop Supervisors
    CAMERON WALDBAUER, GORD DAVIS
Key Special Effects Assistant.........KIM MORTENSEN
Special Effects Buyer...........................BECKY BATES
Special Effects Supervisor .....ANDREW VERHOEVEN
Special Effects Assistants ....JASON DOLAN,
    ADRIAN FISHER, DAN CLARKE, DERRICK ROCKHILL
Special Effects Fabricators....................ATTILA VASKI,
    BOB PRICE, MARTY HUCULIAK,
    JORDAN KIDSTON, DAVE DUNAWAY,
    BRIAN NAKAZAWA, BARRY VALENTINE HEBEIN,
    TREVOR HILL, GEOFF TURNER, KEVIN WILLIS,
    WAYNE MAGNISON, ROBERT ROCKHILL,
    FRANZ FRAITZL, GREG BELLAVANCE,
    NIC CURRAGH, ROD QUINN, BRUNO MAGANIC
Special Effects Riggers ....PERRY BECKHAM,
    STEVE KNIGHT, RAFAEL SOLA,
    ANDRÉ DOMINQUEZ, MIKE DOBBIN,
    GRANT SMITH, ALISTAIR KING, REG MILNE,
    GARY MINIELLY
Pyrotechnics Supervisor............STEWART BRADLEY
Pyrotechnics Assistants ....TERRY SONDERHOFF,
    STEPHEN T. HEPWORTH, KEVIN JAMES ANDRUSCHAK
24-Frame Video Playback ....KLAUS MELCHIOR
Construction Coordinator ....THOMAS WELLS
Construction Buyer....................G. SCOTT STEWART
Construction Foremen ..JIM BERKEL, WARD GALVIN,
    GARY YORK
Standby Carpenter...........................JOHN KOBYLKA
Lead Carpenters ....JOHN NOEL, TOR BAXTER,
    SCOTT WELLERBRINK, HENRY PARKER,
    CHRIS WILLS, MICHAEL OSBORN RODDICK,
    CHRIS COOPER, DOUGLAS JANG, SAM McMASTER,
    BRIAN SHELL, JOHN DALE, DEAN JOSEPH
    McQUILLEN, MARTIN QUESNEL, DAVID TAIT,
    RALF KRONING, SPENCER STEVENSON
Scenic Carpenters ....HARVEY MOELLER,
    MARK ENNIS, BRENT BERG, WAYNE BINMORE,
    NEALL C. HALINGTEN, PETER SCHULTZ,
    PETER PRINCE, TROY BROLLY, ROY GERVAIS,
    ROBERT WATERBEEK, GREG RIDEOUT,
    J. GEOFF CROSBY

Lead Laborer ....RUSSELL SHIELS
Metal Fabricators ....TONY FIORESE,
    MARIO OROLOGIO, LLOYD SKARSGARD,
    PETER WRAY
Head Model Maker ....GORDON BELLAMY
Model Makers..................................MARK STOPE,
    MICHAEL DALE, ANYA SLADE
Sculptor ....MAREK NORMON
Video Graphics Supervisors ....RICK LUPTON
    GLADYS TONG
Computer Playback............................ROB GRAHAM
Head Scenic Artist ....BARRY KOOTCHIN
Scenic Artists.........PETER SYSOEV, DOUG CURRIE,
    FRANKLIN LEIBEL, VALERIE SHMAKIN,
    STEVHAN BONN, TERESA KELLY, SARA WELLS,
    DRAGAN ZARIC, JANIS LEE, BRENDA BORROWMAN,
    LUBOR CENCAK
Paint Foremen......................................MARIO TOMAS
    PAUL DUFFY
Lead Painters ....MALCOLM MACLEAN
    RONALD VOSKUIL, LARRY OSLAND,
    MARTINE BILODEAU, PETER BRADSHAW,
    SEAN WILL
Standby Painter ....TOM ROBERTSON
Painters..............WALLACE CROSS, LINDA BISHOP,
    BRAD KNULL, JON MARTELL, KAY YAMANAKA,
    JAN REEVES, MARIO BURELLE
Studio Teachers............................ANNIE WILKINSON
    DON MUNROE
Assistant to Bryan Singer ....ALEX GARCIA
Executive Assistant to Ms. Shuler Donner KATHY LISKA
Assistant to Ms Shuler Donner............BILL DURHAM
Assistant to Mr. Winter.................SABINE SCHOPPEL
Assistant to Mr. DeSanto..........MATTHEW GRANGER
Assistant to Mr. Jackman ....ERIN CLUTTON
Assistant to Ms. Berry..........KATHERINE BAFARO
Assistant to Mr. McKellen ....STEVE THOMSON
Assistant to Ms. Janssen ....KARIN TOLSON
Assistant to Ms. Paquin, Mr. Cumming
    and Ms. Romijn-Stamos ....KYLE LEYDIER
Supervising Production Accountant
    ELENA HOLDEN BRESS
Production Accountant ....JAMES T. LINVILLE
First Assistant Accountant......CHRISTIAN FELDHAUS
Construction & SPFX Accountant ..WILLIAM PHILLIPS
Visual Effects Accountant KATHY "GEORGIA" EDWARDS
Payroll Accountant............................SANDI ELLAMS
    SUZANNE CLEMENTS
Assistant Accountants ....MONICA MONTELLA,
    COLETTE JOST, STEFANI ROCKWELL, GLORIA GIBB
Accounting Clerks.............................DAVID KLYPAK,
    JENNIFER GIANNONE, CHRISTOPHER GREEN
Production Assistants ....SPENCER HON LUI,
    ALLISON CRUTHERS, KELI A. MOORE,
    MICHAEL GILBERT, JULIA GAUDETTE,
    BREANNE LARRETT, COLIN HOUSE, IAN DAVIS,
    NICHOLAS "SUPER" BRANDT, TAU FLAGG
Greens Coordinator ....AVO LIVA
Assistant Greens ....JOHN CARR,
    GLENN FOERSTER, JUDY SILVER
Movement Coach.............................TERRY NOTARY
Dialect Coaches.......................................JESS PLATT
    FRANCIE BROWN
Casting Associate ....CAROLINE LIEM
Casting Assistant ....CELESTE MOORE
Canadian Casting by ....COREEN MAYRS
    HEIKE BRANDSTATTER
Extras Casting ....ANDREA BROWN
Extras Coordinator..........................ANDREA HUGHES
Unit Publicists ...JOE EVERETT, PATRICIA JOHNSON
Technical Advisors ..RON BLECKER, ROBERT SNOW
Animal Wrangler...............................MARK DUMAS
Transportation Coordinator ....ROB STEEVES
Transportation Captains ....RORY A. MOFFATT
    GREG HAMILTON
Picture Car Coordinator.....................BOB MACLEAN
Picture Car Wranglers.................RICK RASMUSSEN
    DALE TARRANT
First Assistant Editor..........................DOV SAMUELS

Avid Assistant Editor ....ROGER FENTON
Assistant Editors ....ROBERT F. SHUGRUE JR.,
KRISTINE McPHERSON, MARY MORRISEY,
PAUL PARSONS
First Assistant Editor (Vancouver) BRUCE GIESBRECHT
Assistant Editors (Vancouver)
JASON HUMPHREY DALE, PAUL KLASSEN
Visual Effects Editors ....STEVE RAY MOORE
DERRICK MITCHELL
Assistant Visual Effects Editor......ANDREW LOSCHIN
Post Production Coordinator CHRISTOPHER DOWELL
Post Production Assistant....................JAMIE CLARKE
Supervising Sound Editor.................JOHN A. LARSEN
Sound Mixing...........PAUL MASSEY, D.M. HEMPHILL,
MICHAEL HERBICK
Co-Supervising Sound Editor/Sound Designer
CRAIG BERKEY
Dialogue Editors......SUSAN SHACKELFORD DAWES
JIM BROOKSHIRE
ADR Supervisor ....DONALD SYLVESTER
ADR Editor ....LAURA GRAHAM
Effects Editors ....DAVE KULCZYCKI, ERIK AADAHL
Foley Supervisor...................................JOHN MORRIS
Foley Editors ....STEVE F. PRICE
BRUCE TANIS, M.P.S.E.
First Assistant Sound Editors...................DAVID BURK
BLAKE CORNETT
Foley Stage ...."F" WARNER HOLLYWOOD
Foley Artists ....JOHN ROESCH, ALYSON MOORE,
MARILYN GRAF HUBBARD
Foley Recordist ....SCOTT MORGAN
Post Production Facilities provided by
TWENTIETH CENTURY FOX STUDIOS
Additional Sound Mixing ....JIM BOLT
Recordists ....TIM GOMILLION, DENNIS ROGERS,
MATT PATTERSON
Re-recording Engineers ....TIM McCOLM
WILLIAM STEIN
ADR Mixers ....CHARLEEN RICHARDS,
ROBERT DESCHAINE, C.A.S., ANN HADSELL
ADR Recordists ....DAVID LUCARELLI,
TAMI TREADWELL, CLAUDIA CARLE
ADR Engineer ....DEREK CASARI
ADR Facilities......TODD AO STUDIOS, HOLLYWOOD
Music Editor.......................AMANDA GOODPASTER
Assistant Music Editor...............................ROBB BOYD
Score Conducted by...........DAMON INTRABARTOLO
Score Orchestrated by ....JOHN OTTMAN
DAMON INTRABARTOLO
Additional Orchestrations by..........FRANK MACCHIA,
RICK GIOVINAZZO, CHRISTOPHER TIN,
PIERRE ANDRÉ
Orchestra Contractor......................DEBBI DATZ-PYLE
Music Preparation by JOANN KANE MUSIC SERVICES
Score Recorded and Mixed by............CASEY STONE
Digital Recordist........................KEVIN GLOBERMAN
Score Recorded at THE NEWMAN SCORING STAGE,
TWENTIETH CENTURY FOX
Recordist ....JOHN RODD
Engineer ....BILL TALBOTT
Stage Crew.............TOM STEEL, DAMON TEDESCO
Score Mixed ....SIGNET SOUND
Choir Mistress ....BOBBI PAGE
Choir Arranged by ....DEBORAH LURIE
ADR Stage...TODD AO
Voice Casting ....CHRIS DOWELL
Negative Cutter ....GARY BURRITT
Color Timers..................JIM PASSON, CHRIS REGAN
Title Design.....................................ROBERT DAWSON,
JUSTIN BLAMPIED, SIMON CASSELS
Main Title Composites by ASYLUM VISUAL EFFECTS
Senior Visual Effects Supervisor
NATHAN McGUINNESS
CG Artists ....PINK, YUICHIRO YAMASHITA
Inferno Artist ....JESPER NYBROE
Visual Effects Producer ....LINDSAY BURNETT
CG Producer ....JEFF WERNER
Opticals by ....PACIFIC TITLE
End Titles by ....SCARLET LETTERS

Caterer..........TIVOLI MOTION PICTURE CATERERS
Set Medic ....NANCY KRESS
First Aid/Craft Service Assistants ...GAIL M. ESTRADA
ILDIKO BARRETT
Security Coordinator ....GRAEME TAIT
Security Co-Captain.............................RICK IMESON
Visual Effects Producer............................JOYCE COX
Sequence and Data Supervisor ....BILL MAHER
Sequence Supervisor.................STEVE RAY MOORE
Visual Effects Directors of Photography
ERIC SWENSON, DAVID STUMP
Visual Effects First AC ....DENNIS ROGERS
Visual Effects Data Coordinator..........SEAN NOWLAN
Visual Effects Production Managers
MARICEL PAGULAYAN, PATRICK GOLIER
On Set Coordinator................................TYLER KEHL
Coordinator..BRENDA ILIC
Assistant Sequence Coordinator..WHITNEY KITCHEN
AARON COHEN, JULIA GAUDETTE, TERRI BREED

PLATE UNIT
First Assistant Directors ....ELLA KUTSCHERA
PETER DASHKEWYTCH
Second Assistant Directors ....MINDY HESLIN
ALEXIS HINDE
Third Assistant Directors IAN SAMOIL, DAVE BARON
Camera Operator.....................HARVEY LAROCQUE
Visual Effects First AC Camera ....CHRIS DYSON
PETER MITCHNICK
Visual Effects Second AC Camera JUSTIN BERGLER,
ROB KATZ, THOMAS YEARDLEY, SCHANE GODON
Hot Head Technician............................CHRIS WALSH

MOTION CONTROL
Motion Control Technician..............CRAIG SHUMARD
Motion Control Operator ....ERIC PASCARELLI
Video Assist ....DARREN ROBERTSON
MICHAEL UGUCCIONE
Gaffer...JOHN DECKER
Best Boy ....NELSON CASEY
Generator Operators ....MIKE NELL, TOM WALDMAN,
JOHN PIROZAK, FULVIO TODESCO
Key Grip...TOM WALLACE
Dolly Op...PHILIPPE PALU
Best Boy ....JESSIE OLIVER
Grips ....ROBERT BANDA, RYAN COX
Camera Crane Tech ....CRAIG KELLY
Scrip Supervisors......................................KEN FRISS,
PATTY ROBERTSON, SANDI CAMERON
Visual Effects Assistants (Vancouver)
NEACOL BOOTH, GORD DUNICK, MADISON
GRAIE, SHANDY LASHLEY, GORDON WEISKE
Visual Effects Assistants (Los Angeles) TRISTA WAHL,
TOM DU HAMEL, KIRSTIE PALMER
First Aid/Craft Service.........LOUISE HETHERINGTON
MAUREEN YOUNG
Transport Captains ....KEN MARSDEN
ANDREW O'BRAY
Caterers ....CINEMA SCENES
CAL-B-QUES

MINIATURE UNIT
Line Producer.............................JOHN H. RADULOVIC
Director of Photography ....DAVE DRZEWIECKI
Production Coordinator ....NIKKI PARSONS
Production Accountant ....MARILYN TASSO
Assistant Production Accountant ....JIM GARRETT
Payroll Accountant ....JESS NUNEZ
Assistant Director ....GREGG GOLDSTONE
First Assistant Camera ....CHUCK BEMIS,
NED MARTIN, PETER SCHMITT, JAMES THIBO
Second Assistant Camera..................BENNETT CERF
Gaffer...DENNIS CLARK
Best Boys Electric ....DAVE SEXTON
STEVE HODGE, DAVE MUSSELMAN, JOERI WONG
Key Grip...MARK ROEMMICH
Best Boys Grip.........................MARK NAVARRETTE,
BRIAN BERLIN, CHUCK CRIVIER
Equipment Manager ....MARK CHRISTOFFERSEN
Camera Equipment Manager ....DAN GINDROZ

Location Mangers.....................KARLENE GALLEGLY
GARY KESELL
Plate Supervisor ....JEFFREY WILLERTH
Script Suprivsor ....NILA NEUKUM
Special Effects Formen ....JOHN STIRBER,
ROY DOWNEY, CHARLES COOKE,
ROY GOODE, STEPHEN HUMPHREY
Transportation Coordinator.........BUSTER KOHLHOFF
Transportation Captain ....TOM ROBERTS
Craft Service ....PAM JOHNSON
Video Assist.....MICHAEL BELIVEAU, GELNN DERRY
Architectural Consultant ....JEFF DEYOE
Production Assistants.........................KEN ENGLAND
ADAM MENDES, CORY NAYLOR, BOB REIF
RUSSELL THOMAS, CHRIS VARGAS, CARL WOLFE

PYRO CREW
Director of Photography ....BARRY WALTON
Assistant Director ....JJ LINSALATA
First Assistant Camera ....PAUL GUGLIEMO
GARY ANDERTON, COLIN CRANE
Crane Operator ....GEORGE DANA
Gaffer...SHANE KELLY
Best Boy Electric ....DON DAVIDSON
Key Grip..JOHN BLACK
Best Boys Grip ....BOBBY IKEDA, TRACI COLLINS,
DON PADILLA, HUGO ELIZONDA, BRETT ELLIOT,
BOBBY MUNOZ

Miniatures by GRANT McCUNE DESIGN, INC.
Model Shop Supervisor ....MONTY SHOOK
Model Shop Design ....JACK EDJOURIAN
Model Shop Engineer...........................BILL SHOURT
Dam Section Foreman ....CORY FAUCHER
Gen. Room Section Foreman ....RAY MOORE
Model Makers ....SCOTT BURTON, ERIC TUCKER,
RICK WON, COREY BURTON,
MARCELLO PETROCELLI

ADDITIONAL PHOTOGRAPHY/AERIAL UNIT
VANCOUVER
Spacecam Camera Operators ....HANS BJERNO
RON GOODMAN
Spacecam Technician..........................ANDREW SYCH
Pilot ....JIM FILIPPONE
ALBERTA
Spacecam Technician ....GERALD GANGER
Aerial Pilot.....................................GILLES LEVEAQUE
Aerial Safety ....JAMES CIESLAK
HAWAII
Directors of Photography ....MICHAEL PRICKETT
RON CONDON
Assistant Camera ....MICHAEL WEISBROD
JEFFREY FLINT
Aerial Pilot..JOSH LANG
Jet Ski Driver................................DEREK DOERNER
NIAGARA FALLS
Spacecam Camera Operator ....STEVE KOSTER
Spacecam Technician...................RALPH MENDOZA
Aerial Pilot..AL CERRULO

Visual Effects and Animation by CINESITE
Visual Effects Supervisor......STEPHEN ROSENBAUM
Visual Effects Producers...............DAVID ROBINSON
TRACY TAKAHASHI
Visual Effects Art Supervisor...............LUBO HRISTOV
Digital Effects Supervisor .....SERGE SRETSCHINSKY
2D Supervisor ....JASON PICCIONI
Digital Effects Production Manager ....
AUDREA TOPPS-HARJO
Visual Effects Coordinators ....BILL MURPHY
TIM CUNNINGHAM, THOMAS CLARY
TOM HENDRICKSON
Production Assistant ....KATHERINE VOGEL
Executive Producer ....SCOTT DOUGHERTY

CEREBRO SEQUENCE
CG Supervisor..............................DAVID SATCHWELL
2D Sequence Supervisor.....................BRIAN LEACH

Lead TD...LYNN BASAS
Lead Effects TD...............................BILL LA BARGE
Lead FX Animation TD ....REMO BALCELLS
CG Effects TD's..........ERNIE RINARD, KEN IBRAHIM,
　　OSCAR CASTILLO, ANTHONY SERENIL,
　　GAVIN GUERRA, DAVID WAINSTAIN
CG Effects Animators...........................JEFF BENOIT,
　　ANDY TOMANDL, ROB OSTIR, ROBERT CHAPIN
CG Animators.......BRIAN BURKES, SCOTT HOLMES
CG Modeler..MAXX OKAZAKI
Lead Lighter...LYNDON LI
Lighters ....BILLY BROOKS, JAMES CITRON,
　　WAYNE VINCENZI, ERIC TABLADA, ANDY CHEN

NIGHTCRAWLER SEQUENCE
CG Supervisor ....GREGORY ANDERSON
2D Sequence Supervisor ....DAVID LINGENFELSER
Lead TD..VIJOY GADDIPATI
Animation Supervisor..........................CHRIS BAILEY
Character Animators...........................JAMES PARRIS,
　　ANGELA JONES, KENNY SUTHERLAND
　　JOE MANDIA
CG Effects Animators ....ANDREW GAUVREAU,
　　MICHAEL EDLUND, ANDY HOFMAN,
　　DAVID TANNER, BRIAN DAVIS
Lighter ....PATTY FRAZIER

PHENOMENA SEQUENCE
CG Supervisor.....................................ARNON MANOR
2D Sequence Supervisor.......................KAMA MOIHA
Senior TD's...GOKHAN KISACIKOGIU, KEVIN SMITH

CG Effects Animators ....KEVIN SHEEDY,
　　CRAIG "X-RAY" HALPERIN, DAVID DAVIES,
　　DEAN SADAMUNE, BJORN ZIPPRICH, ANDY KING
Shader TD ....LIZA KEITH
Lighters....................RAJI KODJA, DANTE TANTOCO
Compositors...CHRIS LANCE, SERENA NARAMORE,
　　MICHAEL HARBOUR, CRAIG MATHIESON,
　　BRAIN ADAMS, CHRIS CIAMPA, JIM GREEN,
　　CORNELIA MAGAS, MICHAEL MILLER,
　　ADAM MOURA, KIM PEPE, KATIE TUCKER-FICO
Inferno Artists................................RENEE CHAMBLIN
　　TRAVIS BAUMANN
Paint Supervisor...............................CORINNE POOLER
Digital Painters ....VALERIE McMAHON,
　　ARKAY HUR, DANNY ALBANO
Roto Supervisor................................LEA C. LAMBERT
Roto Artists........KRISTINE LANKENAU, WALLY CHIN
Tracking Supervisor.......................RANDY BAHNSEN
Trackers...................NICOLE HERR, MICHAEL KARP,
　　ANDY SILVESTRI, MICHAEL GUTTMAN,
　　BRIAN H. BURKS
Matte Painter...................................RONALD CRABB
Texture Painter...................................JUSTINE SAGAR
Color Imaging Supervisor ....JEFFREY KALMUS
Senior Visual Effects Editor..............PAUL HOWARTH
Visual Effects Editor................................STEVE RHEE
Avid Editor ....KEVIN LANEAVE
Research Scientist ....JERRY TESSEDORF
Senior Systems Administrator..........ROBERT MANCE
Lead Production Support ....CHRIS SERENIL
Systems Administrators ....SCOTT LORD
　　MARK SARTE
Junior Engineer....................ERIC NEWELL-LAVIGNE
Production Manager.........................RALPH DENSON
3D Manager..............................JEFFREY BAKSINSKI
2D Manager................................KEN LITTLETON
Digital Asset Manager......................VINCE LAVARES
3D Render TD.....................DANTÉ QUINTANA
3D Technical Assistant Supervisor ROBERT COQUIA, JR.
2D Technical Assistant Supervisor ...TONY SGUEGLIA
Digital Imaging Coordinator ....RICK BENOIT
Digital Imaging Operators ....KEVIN SCHWAB
　　DALE STELLY
Projectionist ....DAVID SLAUGHTER
Vault Manager ....DENNIS SOLANO
VP Production ....DANIEL J. LOMBARDO
Bid Producer..................................DAPHNE DENTZ

Senior Staffing Manager ....ROBIN THOMPKINS
Office Manager ....PAULETTE LORENZO-HONORÉ
Production Accountant.........................CARLA SIERRA

Special Visual Effect by RHYTHM & HUES, INC.
Visual Effects Supervisor ....RICHARD HOLLANDER
Visual Effects Producer ....LISA GOLDBERG
Digital Effects Supervisor ....MARK RODAHL
Compositing Supervisor ....EDWIN RIVERA
Lighting Supervisor......................DEBBIE PASHKOFF
Design Supervisor ....MIKE MEAKER

Augmentation Room Sequence Supervisor
　　SEAN McPHERSON
Digital Effects Producers..........EDWARD P. BUSCH III
　　SERGE RIOU
Visual Effects Coordinators............STEVE PIMENTAL
　　RYAN POLLREISZ
Digital Coordinators ....JOSHUA FERTIK,
　　PATRICK D. HURD, PATRICK McCORMACK
Production Assistant...................FRANK ANNUNZIATA
Lead Compositor ....CRAIG SIMMS
Compositors .....TONY BARRAZA, CHRIS BERGMAN,
　　ANITA BEVELHEIMER, JEFFREY CASTEL DE ORO,
　　SHELLAINE CORWEL, BETSY COX MCPHERSON,
　　BERTHA GARCIA, LAURA HANIGAN,
　　JENNIFER A. HOWARD, JIMMY JEWELL,
　　PERRY KASS, MATT KELLY, HOIYUE "HARRY" LAM,
　　SEAN HYAN-IN LEE, MATT LINDER,
　　JEREMY NELLIGAN, TONY NOEL,
　　JONATHAN ROBINSON, MARC RUBONE,
　　JOE SALAZAR, JEFF WELLS,
　　MATTHEW T. WILSON, SERKAN ZELZELE
Lead Inferno Artist...............................JOHN HELLER
Inferno Artists.....................KENNETH AU, TIM BIRD,
　　YUKIKO ISHIWATA
Matte Painters.....................MARTHA SNOW MACK,
　　LOPSIE SCHWARTZ, BOB SCIFO,
　　MATTHEW SHUMWAY
Lead Animator.....................................DANNY SPECK
Animators.................GLENN RAMOS, JASON IVIMEY
Lead Lighters ..GREGORY YEPES, RAYMOND CHEN
Lighting Set-Up TD ....KARL HERBST
Lighters ....AMIE SLATE, ANDY GARCIA,
　　FREDERIC SOUMAGNAS, GEE YEUNG,
　　GEORGIA CANO, JASON BAYEVER,
　　JONATHAN MEIER, JON AGHASSIAN,
　　JUDE ADAMSON, MIKE ROBY,
　　SALAR SALEH, TOM CAPIZZI
X-Jet Prelighter....................MARY LYNN MACHADO
Texture Painters.................................NORI KANEKO
　　MICHELLE DENIAUD
Effects Lead ....MIKE O'NEAL
Tornado Effects Lead ....DOUG BLOOM
Effects TDs ....AARON JAMES McCOMAS,
　　ANDERS ERICSON, ALFRED URRUTIA,
　　ANDY SHENG, ANTOINE DURR, CALEB HOWARD,
　　CHRIS RODA, CHRISTOPHER ROMANO,
　　DAN SMICZEK, HIDEKI OKANOJAMES ATKINSON,
　　JEFF WOLVERTON, JON-JON MA, JULIUS YANG,
　　MARK A. McGUIRE, MICHAEL LAFAVE,
　　SCOTT TOWNSEND, STU MINTZ, TOMAS ROSENFELDT
Modelers..........GREGORY GALLIANI, CRAIG CHUN,
　　WEI HO
Animation Set-Up ....JELENA Z. ERCEG
Tracking Supervisor.....................SAMUEL L. NUNEZ
Trackers ....DEAN RASMUSSEN,
　　JUDAH KONIGSBERG, LULU J. SIMON,
　　MARK D. WELSER, RICHARD J. DAVENPORT,
　　VIVIANA PALACIOS
Paint/Roto Artists.......................SUSANA BENTSEN,
　　MIKE FREVENT, BILL GEORGIOU,
　　ANNE H. HERMES, VERONICA HERNANDEZ,
　　MARVIN F. JONES, BILL SCHAEFFER,
　　RICHARD B. STAY
Previz Artist ....BUD MYRICK
Pipeline Support ....MUNIRA M. BHAIJI
Editor ....ZEKE MORALES
Assistant Editor ....DEBORAH PHILLIPS

Scan/Record Operator ....JEFFREY CILLEY
Render I/O Coordinator.............JUSTIN DOMINGUEZ
Education ....ALEX KO
Facilities Supervisor ....JEFF EDEKER
Hardware Technician ....FRANK MURILLO
System Administrator ....KEVIN TENGAN
System Operator....................................JEANNIE YIP
Software Engineer.........................IVAN NEULANDER

Special Visual Effects by KLEISER-WALCZAK
Visual Effects Supervisor ....FRANK E. VITZ
Visual Effects Producer.................MOLLY WINDOVER
Modeling and Effects Lead ....KEVIN NOONE
Texture and Lighting Lead..........LEONARDO QUILES
Lead Compositor ....EDWARDO MENDEZ
2D Shot Supervisor........................MARY E. NELSON
Modeling, Texturing, Lighting Artists
　MICHAEL COMLY, PATRICK FINLEY, DAVE KINTNER
　　ERIK PAYNTER, TRAVIS G. PINSONNAULT
Character and Morph Animation..........DERALD HUNT,
　　GREG LEMON, SIMON SHERR
Compositors ....SVETLA BELCHEVA
　　KATHARINE EVANS, MARC MORISSETTE
　　LEAH NALL, ANDY TANGUAY
Effects Developer ....DANIEL ROIZMAN
Effects Programmer ....BEN ANDERSEN
Render Manager............CHRISTOPHER M. ENGLISH
Editing/Data Managerment.............SLAVICA PANDZIC
Systems Administration ....JOEL FEDER

Pre-Visualization and Post Effects by FRANTIC FILMS
Visual Effects Supervisor ....CHRIS BOND
Visual Effects Producer ....KEN ZORNIAK
2D Supervisors ..DARREN WALL, SHANE DAVIDSON
3D Supervisor...................................CONRAD DUECK
Visual Effecst Coordinator ....RANDAL SHORE
3D Artist ....CHAD WIEBE
Programmer ....LASZLO SEBO
2D Compositor ....JASON BOOTH
Visual Effects TD ....JASON COBILL

Special Visual Effects by PACIFIC TITLE
Visual Effects Supervisor...................DAVID SOSALLA
Executive Producer...............................JOE GARERI
Inferno Compositors PATRICK PHILLIPS, BOB WIATR
Cineon Compositor ....JENNIFER LAW STUMP
Digital Painters ....GEORGE GERVAN,
　　RICHARD GERVAN, PATRICK KENEEN
Digital Coordinator ....JAMES D. TITTLE
Digital I/O ....JOHN MORCOS, BRIAN MILLER,
　　RICK KIM, STEVE LANGIUS

Special Visual Effects by HAMMERHEAD PRODUCTIONS
Visual Effects Supervisor ....REBECCA MARIE
Animator..JUSTIN JONES

Special Visual Effects by CIS HOLLYWOOD
Visual Effects Supervisor ....BRYAN HIROTA
Visual Effects Producer.........................JULIE OROSZ
Digital Compositing Supervisor.............GREG LIEGEY
Compositors ..PATRICK KAVANAUGH, MARC NANJO
Lead CG Artist ....DIANA MIAO
CG Artist...AMY GARBACK
Production Coordinator ....TOM SLOVICK
R&D Supervisor....................................CHRIS ALLEN
R&D Programmer ....KYLE YAMAMOTO
CG Artist...JOHN CASSELLA
General Manager ....DONALD FLY
Systems..MATT ASHTON
Accounting ....MARYJANE LAYANI

Special Visual Effects by PIXEL MAGIC
Visual Effects Supervisor ..RAYMOND McINTYRE, JR.
General Manager ....RAY SCALICE
Executive Producer.........................BONNIE KANNER
Digital Effects Supervisor ....VICTOR DiMICHINA
Digital Compositors.....................................JOE DUBS,
　　ALFREDO RAMIREZ, BRUCE HARRIS

CREDITS

Special Visual Effect by VCE.COM/PETER KURAN
3D Supervisor ....KEVIN KUTCHAVER
3d Effects Lead ....JOHN GIBBONS
Composite Supervisor...............PHILIP CARBONARO
Composite Roto Artist ....PAM VICK
Digital Compositor ....KURT WILEY
Digital Matte Painter...........................CARLIN KMETZ
Visual Effects Editorial.............................JO MARTIN

Special Visual Effects by 4WARD PRODUCTIONS, INC.

Scanning and Modeling by LIDAR SERVICES, INC.

Digital Pre-Visualization Animatics
Pre-Visual Artists ....RPIN SUWANNATH
IMAGE ENGINE
Story Board Artist ....THOMAS LEY

SECOND UNIT

Second Unit Director ....BRIAN SMRZ
Director of Photography ....GARY CAPO
Unit Manager ....YVONNE MELVILLE
First Assistant Director ....MATT REBENKOFF
Second Assistant Directors...............FIONA WINNING
EDDY SANTOS
Third Assistant Director................MISHA BUKOWSKI
Trainee Assistant Director....................JANE TALBOT
Set Decorator ....ROSS WAHL
Script Supervisors ....JEAN BEREZIUK
TERRY MURRAY
Camera Operator/Steadicam ....DAVID CRONE
Steadicam Operator ....JIMMY MURO
A Camera First Assistants ....DOUG LAVENDER,
ARIS GEORGIOPOULOS, BRAD PETERMAN
A Camera Second Assistants...........KEVIN HAVERTY
SHINPEI OTSUKI
B Camera Operator ....PAUL MITCHNICK
B Camera First Assistant....................IAN SEABROOK
B Camera Second Assistant Trainee
CARY LALONDE, DAVID WESLEY KYLE
Video Assist ....CLINT PAGLARO, DAVID JOSHI
Sound Mixers ....TIM RICHARDSON
WILLIAM BUTLER
Boom Person...................................SCOTT CARROLL
Gaffer...STEPHEN JACKSON
Best Boys-Electric...........................SHAWN MILSTED
TERRY P. CALHOUN
Dimmer Board Operators VANCE VEGAS SALVALAGGIO
SEAN OXENBURY
Generator Operators ....ROGER BAILEY,
GILBERT JAMAULT, DAVID GOYER
Electricians ....CHRISTOPHER PRICE,
SCOTT MITCHELL, VINCE LAXTON, LEE MILLER,
DOUG BROWN, RON ZITTLAU
Key Grip...JOHN LE ROY
Best Boy...DEREK LEROY
Dolly Grips ....BRIAN SCANNEL, TODD HLAGI
Grips ....TONY BECK, KEN HEMPHILL,
PAUL MOHR, DEAN RECA
Property Master ....DEAN EILERTON
Props...DOUG FOREMAN
CHRIS "SHARPIE" SHARP

Standby Carpenter.................................CHRIS WILLS
Standby Painter ....DUSTY KELLY
Standby Greens...........................JOSEPHINE BLEUER
Costume Supervisor...................BONNIE SUTHERLAND
Costumer ....KELLY BRUHM
Key Make-Up Artist ....JOANN FOWLER
Assistant Make-Up Artists ....KRISTA YOUNG,
TOBY LINDALA, WIN KONIJN
Key Hair Stylist ....KANDACE LOEWEN
Assistant Hair Stylist ....CINDY BURWASH
Special Effects Coordinator....................GORD DAVIS
Special Effects Best Boy ....CLAYTON SCHEIRER
Special Effects Assistants ....COLIN NASO,
JOHN WILKINSON, CLANCY SCHEIRER,
CHRIS DAVIS, PAUL NOEL, WAYNE SZYBUNKA
Aerial Coordinator ....JIM FILIPPONE
Vertol Pilots ....KIRK SUNTER, JEFF SIM
Vertol Maintenance...............................KIRK RODDIE
SASHA LYTTAK
Spacecam Operator ....HANS BJERNO
Spacecam Technician........................ANDREW SYCH
Helicopter Safety ....DENIS RIGO
Camera Pilot...............................GILLES LEVESQUE
Camera Cranes & Dollies by.....CHAPMAN/LEONARD
STUDIO EQUIPMENT, INC.

Remote Cranes supplied by
TELESCOPIC CAMERA CRANE LTD.

SOUNDTRACK AVAILABLE ON SUPERB RECORDS

SONGS

DIES IRAE FROM MOZART'S
REQUIEM IN D MINOR, K.626
Written by Wolfgang Amadeus Mozart
Courtesy of FirstCom Music Inc.

EVOLUTION EXHIBIT
Written and Performed by Christopher Tin

NEWS THEME
Written and Performed by Christopher Tin

CENTER OF THE SUN
Written by Annie Danielewski and Rhys Fulber
Performed by Conjure One featuring Poe
Courtesy of Nettwerk Productions

EINE KLEINE NACHTMUSIK, ROMANZE
Written by Wolfgang Amadeus Mozart
Performed by The National Arts Centre Orchestra,
conductor Mario Bernardi
Courtesy of CBC Records/Les Disques SRC

GAME SHOW NETWORK ORIGINAL
PROGRAM END CUE
Courtesy of Game Show Network, LLC

PASTORAL LANDS
Written and Performed by William Loose
Courtesy of Marc Ferrari/Tinseltown Music Library

BYE BYE BYE
Written by Andreas Carlsson, Kristian Lundin and
Jacob Schulze, Performed by N'SYNC
Courtesy of Jive Records

SPORTS JAM
Written and Performed by Christopher Tin

MOZART'S SONATA K545
Written by Mozart Amadeus Mozart
Performed by Don Great
Courtesy of Marc Ferrari/Tinseltown Music Library

THE PRODUCERS WISH TO THANK THE FOLLOW-
ING FOR THEIR ASSISTANCE:
BRITISH COLUMBIA FILM COMMISSION
VANCOUVER FILM STUDIOS LTD.
CITY OF VANCOUVER, B.C.
CITY OF SURREY, B.C.
CITY OF COLWOOD, B.C.
ROYAL ROADS UNIVERSITY
HATLEY PARK
ST. ANDREW'S-WESLEY CHURCH
WHITE HOUSE HISTORICAL ASSOCIATION
TRANSALTA UTILITIES CORPORATION
B.C. HYDRO
ALBERTA COMMUNITY DEVELOPMENT
ROYAL TYRRELL MUSEUM
DIRECTORS GUILD OF CANADA
B.C. COUNCIL OF FILM UNIONS
PANAVISION CANADA
EP CANADA INC.
MAZDA MOTOR CORPORATION
BASKIN ROBBINS
DR. PEPPER
THE COFFEE BEAN AND TEA LEAF

Spacecam Aerial Camera System
Provided by SPACECAM SYSTEMS, INC

Lighting and Grip Equipment
WILLIAM F. WHITE LIMITED

Filmed with remote cranes and heads from
PANAVISION REMOTE SYSTEMS

Dailies by ALPHACINE

Color and Prints by DELUXE®

Filmed with PANAVISION® Cameras and Lenses

KODAK FILM STOCK

Approved No. 39703
MOTION PICTURE ASSOCIATION OF AMERICA

Copyright © 2003 Twentieth Century Fox Film Corporation in all
territories except Brazil, Italy, Korea, Japan and Spain.

Copyright © 2003 TCF Hungary Film Rights Exploitation
Limited Liability Company and Twentieth Century Fox Film
Corporation in Brazil, Italy, Korea, Japan and Spain.

Twentieth Century Fox Film Corporation is the author of this
motion picture for purposes of copyright and other laws.

The events, characters and firms depicted in this photoplay are
fictitious. Any similarity to actual persons, living or dead, or to
actual events or firms is purely coincidental.

Ownership of this motion picture is protected by copyright and
other applicable laws, and any unauthorized duplication, distri-
bution or exhibition of this motion picture could result in criminal
prosecution as well as civil liability.

ACKNOWLEDGMENTS

Publisher Esther Margolis of Newmarket Press wishes to thank the following for their special contributions to this book:

At Twentieth Century Fox: Bryan Singer, Alex Garcia, Ralph Winter, Lauren Shuler Donner, David Gorder, Tom DeSanto, Debbie Olshan, Chrissy Quesada, Kathy Liska, Gianna Babando, Richard Prolsdorfer, John Myhre, Tamara Deverell, Adam Grell, Hunter Hancock, Matt Grange, William Cameron; special thanks to Guy H. Dyas for supplying detailed notes on the production designs, to Oscar Richards for the Bryan Singer introduction, and to Peter Sanderson for enriching our knowledge of the X-Men, and Christopher Measom for his additional text; Timothy Shaner, Dan Harris, Amanda Roth, Monty Shook, John Radulovic, Dominique Dyas, St. Mark's Comics, Pete Larson, *Cinefex Magazine*; and at Newmarket Press, Frank DeMaio, Tom Perry, Keith Hollaman, Shannon Berning, Kelli Taylor, Chris Cousino, Harry Burton, and Heidi Sachner.

160.X2